PROTECTING & PROSPERING
In Uncertain Times

Created by the CopyPeople.com[1]

All rights reserved.

Copyright © 2024 onwards .

By reading this book, you agree to the following Terms and Conditions:

All rights to this book are retained by CopyPeople.com[2]. No part of this book may be reproduced in any form, including photostat, microfilm, xerography, or any other means, without written permission from CopyPeople.com[3]. Brief excerpts may be used in published reviews.

This book is for entertainment purposes only and does not provide legal, accounting, health, relationship, or professional advice. For professional assistance, please consult a qualified expert.

By purchasing and reading this book, you acknowledge and agree to this disclaimer.Thank you for your understanding and support.

- **Get A Free Book At:** https://free.copypeople.com

[4]

---

1. https://copypeople.com/

2. https://copypeople.com/

3. https://copypeople.com/

4. https://free.copypeople.com

Table of Contents

Embracing Uncertainty: A Family's Journey

Embracing Uncertainty: A Family's Journey

In the face of a recession, embracing uncertainty becomes a vital part of navigating financial and emotional stability for families. A recession introduces a range of challenges, from job insecurity to fluctuating investments, which can impact every aspect of family life. Embracing this uncertainty requires a proactive and adaptable approach, one that strengthens familial bonds while securing financial stability. Here's a roadmap for families to effectively handle the turbulence of a recession.

Understanding the Scope of Uncertainty

Uncertainty during a recession encompasses more than just financial fluctuations; it affects job security, market stability, and even day-to-day living costs. To navigate these challenges effectively, it's crucial for families to first understand the full scope of uncertainty they might face. Start by educating all family members about the economic situation, including its potential impacts on household finances and employment.

Discussing the broader economic landscape helps demystify the situation and reduces anxiety. It also prepares the family for potential changes and fosters a collective sense of readiness. Transparency about financial realities and potential outcomes allows everyone to approach the situation with a clear, informed perspective.

Developing a Unified Financial Strategy

Creating a unified financial strategy is essential for managing a family's finances during a recession. Begin by organizing a family meeting to review and update the household budget. This involves tracking all sources of income, evaluating essential and non-essential expenses, and identifying areas for potential savings.

Implement a conservative approach to budgeting, focusing on reducing discretionary spending and prioritizing essential needs such as housing, utilities, and groceries. Consider setting up a family savings goal that emphasizes building an emergency fund. An emergency fund provides a financial buffer that can cover unexpected expenses or gaps in income.

Adapting to Income Fluctuations

Income fluctuations are a common challenge during a recession. To address this, families should explore various ways to adapt and supplement their income. Encourage family members to identify and leverage any additional skills or talents that could generate extra income. This might include freelance work, part-time jobs, or entrepreneurial ventures.

Diversifying income sources helps mitigate the risk of losing a single income stream and provides additional financial security. Families should also be prepared to adjust their spending patterns based on changes in income. This might involve reassessing and recalibrating the budget regularly to reflect current financial conditions.

Enhancing Family Communication and Support

Effective communication and support are crucial during uncertain times. Openly discussing financial concerns and strategies helps reduce stress and ensures that all family members are on the same page. Establish regular family meetings to review financial status, discuss any changes, and make collective decisions.

Fostering a supportive environment involves acknowledging the emotional impact of financial stress. Encourage family members to express their feelings and concerns openly. Providing emotional support, reassurance, and encouragement helps maintain a positive outlook and strengthens family cohesion.

Investing in Long-Term Stability

While addressing immediate financial concerns is important, investing in long-term stability should not be overlooked. Recessions provide an opportunity to re-evaluate long-term financial goals and make necessary adjustments. Consider revising savings and investment strategies to align with current economic conditions.

Investing in skills and education also contributes to long-term stability. Encouraging family members to pursue further education, vocational training, or skill development enhances their employability and adaptability in a shifting job market. This proactive approach builds a foundation for future financial security.

Cultivating Resilience and Adaptability

Cultivating resilience and adaptability is key to managing the uncertainty of a recession. Families should adopt a flexible mindset, ready to adjust plans and strategies as circumstances evolve. Emphasize the importance of staying informed about economic trends and being prepared to make timely decisions.

Encourage a problem-solving approach to challenges, focusing on finding practical solutions rather than dwelling on difficulties. Building resilience involves fostering a positive outlook and maintaining a sense of hope, even in the face of adversity.

Building Community Connections

Building and maintaining community connections can provide valuable support during uncertain times. Engage with local support networks, community organizations, or social groups that offer resources and assistance. These connections can provide practical help, such as financial aid or job leads, as well as emotional support.

Participating in community activities and volunteering also fosters a sense of belonging and shared purpose. Strengthening these connections not only enhances individual resilience but also contributes to the collective well-being of the community.

By embracing uncertainty with a proactive and adaptable approach, families can navigate the challenges of a recession more effectively. Understanding the scope of uncertainty, developing a unified financial strategy, adapting to income fluctuations, enhancing communication and support, investing in long-term stability, cultivating resilience, and building community connections are all critical components of a successful journey through economic adversity.

Building a Resilient Foundation at Home

Building a Resilient Foundation at Home

During a recession, building a resilient foundation at home becomes essential for maintaining both financial stability and family cohesion. Economic downturns can strain household finances, disrupt routines, and test the strength of familial bonds. Establishing a strong, adaptable foundation helps families navigate these challenges with greater ease and security. Here's how to create a resilient home environment that supports financial stability and emotional well-being.

Creating a Robust Financial Plan

A resilient foundation starts with a well-structured financial plan. Begin by reviewing and updating your household budget to reflect the current economic climate. Track all sources of income and categorize expenses into essential and non-essential. Prioritize essential expenses like housing, utilities, food, and healthcare while identifying areas where non-essential spending can be reduced.

Establish an emergency fund to provide a financial buffer in case of unexpected expenses or income disruptions. Aim to save three to six months' worth of living expenses in a separate, easily accessible account. Regularly contribute to this fund and adjust your budget as needed to ensure it remains aligned with your financial goals.

Securing and Protecting Assets

Securing your home and personal assets is crucial during uncertain times. Review your homeowner's or renter's insurance policy to ensure it provides adequate coverage for potential risks. Consider updating your policy to reflect any changes in the value of your home or belongings.

Invest in home security measures to protect against theft or damage. Install quality locks on doors and windows, and consider adding a security system or surveillance cameras. Maintaining a secure home environment helps prevent additional stress and financial loss during challenging times.

Strengthening Family Communication

Open and honest communication is the cornerstone of a resilient family foundation. Regularly discuss financial matters, including the household budget, savings goals, and any changes in income or expenses. Involving all family members in these discussions fosters a sense of shared responsibility and helps everyone understand the family's financial situation.

Create a safe space for family members to express their concerns and feelings about the recession. Address any fears or anxieties and offer reassurance and support. Regular family meetings can provide a structured forum for discussing challenges, making decisions, and celebrating successes.

Implementing Cost-Saving Measures

Implementing cost-saving measures is a practical way to strengthen your financial foundation. Review recurring expenses and identify opportunities for savings. This might include reducing utility bills through energy-efficient practices, cutting back on non-essential services, or seeking out more affordable alternatives for everyday items.

Consider adopting a more frugal lifestyle by shopping smartly, using coupons, and taking advantage of discounts. Planning meals, reducing food waste, and buying in bulk can also contribute to cost savings. Encourage family members to contribute ideas and participate in cost-saving efforts, reinforcing a sense of teamwork and shared commitment.

Building Emotional and Psychological Resilience

Emotional resilience is as important as financial stability when building a resilient foundation at home. Create a supportive environment where family members can cope with stress and uncertainty. Encourage activities that promote relaxation and well-being, such as exercise, hobbies, and family outings.

Foster a positive outlook by focusing on what can be controlled and taking proactive steps to address challenges. Practice gratitude and celebrate small victories to maintain a hopeful perspective. Building emotional resilience helps families stay grounded and united during tough times.

Developing Long-Term Financial Strategies

Long-term financial strategies are essential for building a stable foundation that can withstand economic fluctuations. Review and adjust your long-term financial goals to align with current circumstances. Consider reallocating investments to safer assets or exploring opportunities for growth in uncertain markets.

Invest in personal development and education to enhance employability and financial security. Encourage family members to acquire new skills or pursue further education that can open up new opportunities and increase earning potential. Long-term planning and strategic investments contribute to ongoing stability and resilience.

Fostering a Sense of Community

Building a sense of community can provide additional support and resources during a recession. Engage with local organizations, support groups, and community networks that offer assistance and encouragement. Volunteering and participating in community events foster a sense of belonging and connection.

Developing relationships with neighbors and local businesses can also provide practical support, such as sharing resources or exchanging services. A strong community network enhances overall resilience and provides a valuable support system during challenging times.

By focusing on creating a robust financial plan, securing assets, strengthening communication, implementing cost-saving measures, building emotional resilience, developing long-term strategies, and fostering a sense of community, families can build a resilient foundation at home. This comprehensive approach helps ensure financial stability and emotional well-being, enabling families to navigate the uncertainties of a recession with greater confidence and security.

Financial Strategies for Tough Times

Financial Strategies for Tough Times

Navigating personal finance and maintaining family stability during a recession requires thoughtful financial strategies. Economic downturns can lead to job losses, decreased income, and increased financial stress. Implementing effective strategies can help families manage their finances, minimize stress, and ensure long-term stability. Here's a guide to financial strategies that can help you weather tough times.

Revising Your Budget

The first step in managing finances during a recession is to revise your household budget. Start by tracking all sources of income, including any side gigs or freelance work. Categorize expenses into essentials (e.g., mortgage or rent, utilities, groceries, healthcare) and non-essentials (e.g., dining out, subscriptions, entertainment).

Prioritize essential expenses to ensure that your basic needs are met. Review non-essential spending and identify areas where cuts can be made. Implement a zero-based budgeting approach, where every dollar is allocated to a specific expense or savings goal. This method helps you make intentional financial decisions and avoids overspending.

Building and Maintaining an Emergency Fund

An emergency fund is a critical component of financial resilience. Aim to save three to six months' worth of living expenses in a separate, easily accessible account. This fund acts as a financial cushion during periods of income disruption or unexpected expenses.

If you don't have an emergency fund yet, start by setting aside a small, manageable amount from each paycheck. Automate transfers to your emergency fund to ensure consistent contributions. Even modest savings can accumulate over time and provide a valuable safety net.

Reducing and Managing Debt

During a recession, managing and reducing debt becomes even more important. High-interest debt, such as credit card balances, can quickly become unmanageable. Focus on paying down high-interest debt first while making minimum payments on other debts. This approach, known as the debt avalanche method, minimizes interest payments and accelerates debt reduction.

Consider consolidating or refinancing debt to secure lower interest rates and reduce monthly payments. Explore options such as personal loans or balance transfer credit cards. If you're struggling with debt, seek help from credit counseling services or financial advisors who can provide guidance and support.

Exploring Additional Income Streams

Diversifying your income sources can provide extra financial stability during tough times. Look for opportunities to generate additional income, such as freelance work, part-time jobs, or gig economy tasks. Online platforms offer various options, from writing and graphic design to tutoring and virtual assistance.

Identify and leverage any skills or hobbies that can be monetized. For example, if you're skilled in crafting, consider selling handmade items online. Offering consulting or coaching services based on your expertise can also provide supplementary income.

Prioritizing Essential Expenses

When finances are tight, it's crucial to prioritize spending on essential needs. Focus on expenses that are critical for your well-being, such as housing, utilities, food, and healthcare. Temporarily defer or reduce spending on non-essential items like vacations, luxury goods, and entertainment.

Create a hierarchy of needs to guide spending decisions. Ensure that you cover basic necessities before allocating funds to non-essential purchases. This approach helps you manage financial constraints while maintaining essential services and products.

Reviewing and Adjusting Investments

Recessions can impact investment values, so it's essential to review and adjust your investment strategy. Assess your investment portfolio and consider reallocating assets to more stable or conservative investments. Diversify your investments to reduce risk and avoid overexposure to any single asset class.

Consult with a financial advisor to evaluate your investment strategy and make adjustments based on current economic conditions. They can help you navigate market fluctuations and develop a plan that aligns with your financial goals and risk tolerance.

Utilizing Available Resources and Assistance

During a recession, various resources and assistance programs can provide support. Research local, state, and federal programs that offer financial aid, food assistance, housing support, or unemployment benefits. Many organizations provide temporary relief and resources to help families manage financial challenges.

Apply for assistance programs as needed and stay informed about eligibility criteria and application processes. Accessing available resources can help alleviate financial pressure and provide support during periods of economic hardship.

Maintaining Financial Flexibility

Flexibility is key to managing finances during a recession. Be prepared to adjust your financial strategies as circumstances change. Regularly review your budget, emergency fund, and debt management plan to ensure they remain aligned with your current situation.

Adopt a proactive approach to financial planning by staying informed about economic trends and anticipating potential changes. Being adaptable helps you respond effectively to new challenges and maintain financial stability.

By implementing these financial strategies—revising your budget, building an emergency fund, reducing debt, exploring additional income streams, prioritizing essential expenses, adjusting investments, utilizing available resources, and maintaining flexibility—you can better navigate the financial challenges of a recession. These measures help ensure your family's financial stability and resilience, providing a foundation for weathering tough times with greater confidence and security.

Strengthening Bonds: Family Support Systems

Strengthening Bonds: Family Support Systems

During a recession, maintaining family stability and financial well-being hinges on robust support systems. Economic downturns can strain relationships and create additional stress, making it essential for families to strengthen their support networks. By fostering a cohesive and supportive family environment, you can navigate financial challenges more effectively and safeguard emotional health. Here's how to build and enhance family support systems during tough times.

Promoting Open Communication

Effective communication is the cornerstone of a strong family support system. Openly discussing financial issues, including the impacts of the recession, helps to align expectations and foster mutual understanding. Schedule regular family meetings to address financial matters, share concerns, and discuss strategies for managing expenses and income.

Encourage every family member to voice their thoughts and feelings about the current situation. Create a non-judgmental space where everyone feels comfortable expressing their concerns and ideas. This open dialogue helps prevent misunderstandings and reinforces a sense of unity and shared purpose.

Fostering Emotional Support

Economic stress can take a toll on emotional well-being. It's crucial to offer emotional support to all family members. Acknowledge and validate each person's feelings of anxiety, frustration, or uncertainty. Provide reassurance and encouragement to help alleviate stress and maintain a positive outlook.

Engage in activities that promote emotional well-being, such as family bonding exercises, mindfulness practices, or simple acts of kindness. Encourage each other to pursue hobbies, exercise, or other activities that provide relief from stress. Emotional support strengthens resilience and enhances the overall stability of the family unit.

Setting Shared Goals and Expectations

Setting shared goals and expectations helps align family efforts and fosters a sense of collective responsibility. Establish common objectives related to budgeting, savings, and debt management. Discuss how each family member can contribute to achieving these goals, whether through reducing personal spending, finding additional income sources, or supporting each other emotionally.

Creating a family mission statement or set of guiding principles can help reinforce these goals and provide a sense of direction. Regularly review progress toward these objectives and adjust plans as needed to reflect changing circumstances.

Building a Support Network

In addition to internal family support, external support networks can provide valuable assistance during a recession. Connect with friends, neighbors, and community organizations that offer resources or emotional support. Joining local support groups or online communities focused on financial management or emotional well-being can provide additional perspectives and resources.

Leverage community resources, such as food banks, financial assistance programs, or counseling services, to address specific needs. Building a network of trusted individuals and organizations creates a broader safety net and reduces the isolation that can accompany financial hardship.

Encouraging Mutual Assistance

Encouraging mutual assistance within the family strengthens support systems and fosters a collaborative environment. Each family member can play a role in helping others, whether by offering practical help, such as childcare or household chores, or by providing emotional support and encouragement.

Create a system for rotating responsibilities or sharing tasks to reduce individual stress and workload. This collaborative approach ensures that no one person is overwhelmed and reinforces the sense of teamwork and solidarity within the family.

Developing Conflict Resolution Skills

Financial stress can sometimes lead to conflicts or disagreements. Developing effective conflict resolution skills is essential for maintaining family harmony. Encourage open and respectful discussions when disagreements arise, focusing on finding solutions rather than assigning blame.

Practice active listening and empathy to understand different perspectives and address underlying issues. Seeking compromise and focusing on common goals helps resolve conflicts constructively and strengthens family relationships.

Implementing a Family Support Plan

A family support plan outlines strategies for managing financial and emotional challenges together. Develop a plan that includes specific actions, such as budgeting techniques, financial goals, and support mechanisms. Ensure that the plan is flexible and adaptable to changing circumstances.

Review and update the support plan regularly to reflect new developments or changes in the family's situation. This proactive approach helps maintain focus and ensures that the family remains united in their efforts to navigate the recession.

Encouraging Resilience and Positivity

Resilience and positivity are crucial for maintaining stability during tough times. Encourage family members to adopt a resilient mindset, focusing on solutions rather than dwelling on problems. Celebrate small victories and milestones, and maintain a positive outlook despite challenges.

Promote practices that build resilience, such as setting realistic goals, practicing gratitude, and maintaining a hopeful perspective. Resilience helps the family adapt to changes and recover from setbacks, strengthening the overall support system.

By promoting open communication, fostering emotional support, setting shared goals, building support networks, encouraging mutual assistance, developing conflict resolution skills, implementing a support plan, and encouraging resilience, families can strengthen their support systems during a recession. A robust support network not only helps manage financial challenges but also reinforces family bonds and emotional well-being, ensuring greater stability and cohesion through uncertain times.

Navigating Emotional Turbulence Together

Navigating Emotional Turbulence Together

During a recession, families often face not just financial stress but significant emotional turbulence as well. Economic downturns can trigger anxiety, uncertainty, and strain relationships. Effectively navigating this emotional turbulence together is crucial for maintaining family stability and supporting each other through challenging times. Here's how families can address and manage emotional challenges as a united front.

Acknowledging and Addressing Emotional Impact

The first step in navigating emotional turbulence is acknowledging its existence and impact. Recessions can lead to heightened stress, fear about the future, and feelings of helplessness. Encourage open discussions about these emotions within the family. Validate each person's feelings and recognize that it's normal to experience a range of emotions during difficult times.

Create a safe space where family members feel comfortable sharing their concerns and fears. This openness helps prevent bottled-up emotions from escalating into conflicts and supports mutual understanding. Addressing emotional challenges head-on reinforces the sense of solidarity and collective strength.

Developing Coping Mechanisms

Coping mechanisms are essential for managing stress and maintaining emotional health. Encourage family members to adopt healthy coping strategies, such as engaging in physical activity, practicing mindfulness or meditation, or pursuing hobbies that provide relaxation and joy. Establishing a routine that includes these activities can provide stability and a sense of normalcy amid uncertainty.

Support each other in developing and maintaining individual coping strategies. Share techniques that work for you and be open to trying new methods together. For example, family walks, game nights, or creative projects can offer both relaxation and quality time together.

Building Emotional Resilience

Emotional resilience helps families adapt to stress and bounce back from adversity. Foster resilience by focusing on strengths and positive aspects of the situation. Encourage family members to set achievable goals and celebrate progress, no matter how small. Building a resilient mindset involves recognizing and leveraging your family's collective strengths and resources.

Promote a positive outlook by encouraging gratitude practices. Regularly acknowledge and appreciate the positive elements of your lives, such as supportive relationships or small victories. Gratitude helps shift focus from what's lacking to what's going well, contributing to emotional stability.

Supporting Each Other Through Change

Economic downturns often bring about significant changes, such as job loss or reduced income. Support each other through these transitions by maintaining open lines of communication and offering practical and emotional support. Discuss the implications of changes openly and work together to develop strategies for adapting to new circumstances.

Be patient and empathetic as family members adjust to these changes. Everyone processes transitions differently, and it's important to respect each person's pace and approach. Offer reassurance and encouragement, and work together to find solutions and adjust expectations as needed.

Maintaining Family Connections

Maintaining strong family connections is vital for emotional support. Spend quality time together, engaging in activities that foster bonding and create positive memories. Family dinners, movie nights, and regular check-ins can help maintain a sense of togetherness and provide opportunities for open communication.

Strengthen family relationships by showing appreciation and support. Simple gestures, such as expressing gratitude, offering compliments, or providing a listening ear, contribute to a nurturing environment. Maintaining close connections helps reinforce the family's emotional support network.

Seeking Professional Help

When emotional turbulence becomes overwhelming, seeking professional help can provide additional support. Family counseling or therapy can offer a safe space for addressing emotional issues and developing coping strategies. A mental health professional can provide guidance and techniques for managing stress and improving communication.

Encourage family members to seek individual counseling if needed. Personal therapy can address specific emotional challenges and complement family support efforts. Professional help can be a valuable resource for navigating complex emotions and maintaining mental health during tough times.

Creating a Supportive Environment

Creating a supportive home environment involves both practical and emotional considerations. Ensure that the home is a space where family members feel safe, comfortable, and supported. Encourage open communication, mutual respect, and empathy in daily interactions.

Set aside time for family activities that promote relaxation and bonding. Create a routine that incorporates moments of connection and reflection, helping to maintain emotional stability. A supportive environment enhances overall well-being and strengthens the family's ability to handle stress.

Fostering Mutual Encouragement

Mutual encouragement plays a crucial role in navigating emotional turbulence. Support each other in pursuing personal goals and aspirations, and celebrate each other's achievements. Offer encouragement and affirmation during challenging times, reinforcing the family's collective resilience.

Encourage family members to share their hopes and dreams, and work together to support these aspirations. Mutual encouragement fosters a sense of unity and motivates everyone to persevere through difficulties.

By acknowledging and addressing emotional impacts, developing coping mechanisms, building resilience, supporting each other through change, maintaining connections, seeking professional help, creating a supportive environment, and fostering mutual encouragement, families can navigate emotional turbulence together. This unified approach strengthens emotional bonds and contributes to overall stability, helping families weather the storm of a recession with greater cohesion and support.

Preparing for the Unexpected: Essential Steps

Preparing for the Unexpected: Essential Steps

In a recession, preparing for the unexpected is crucial for maintaining personal finance and family stability. Economic downturns can lead to sudden changes, such as job loss, unexpected expenses, or financial market fluctuations. By taking proactive steps, families can build resilience and safeguard their financial well-being against unforeseen challenges. Here's a guide to essential steps for preparing for the unexpected during uncertain times.

Building a Robust Emergency Fund

An emergency fund acts as a financial buffer during unexpected events. Aim to save three to six months' worth of living expenses in a separate, easily accessible account. This fund provides a safety net for emergencies such as medical expenses, car repairs, or sudden loss of income.

To build your emergency fund, start by setting aside a small, manageable portion of your income each month. Automate transfers to your savings account to ensure consistency. Even incremental contributions can accumulate over time, providing valuable financial security.

Creating a Comprehensive Financial Plan

A comprehensive financial plan helps you prepare for various scenarios, from job loss to large medical bills. Begin by assessing your current financial situation, including income, expenses, assets, and liabilities. Develop a plan that outlines how you will manage your finances in the event of unexpected changes.

Include strategies for reducing expenses, managing debt, and adjusting your budget in response to changing circumstances. Regularly review and update your financial plan to reflect any significant changes in your life or economic conditions.

Securing Adequate Insurance Coverage

Adequate insurance coverage is essential for protecting your family from financial risks. Review your insurance policies, including health, life, disability, and property insurance, to ensure they provide sufficient coverage.

Consider increasing coverage or adding supplemental policies if necessary. For example, disability insurance can provide income replacement if you are unable to work due to illness or injury. Adequate coverage helps mitigate the financial impact of unexpected events and provides peace of mind.

Diversifying Income Sources

Relying on a single source of income can be risky during a recession. Diversify your income streams to reduce financial vulnerability. Explore opportunities for additional income, such as freelance work, part-time jobs, or passive income sources like investments or rental properties.

Identify skills or hobbies that can be monetized and seek out side gigs or freelance opportunities that align with your expertise. Diversifying income helps stabilize your financial situation and provides a buffer against potential job loss or reduced income.

Developing a Debt Management Strategy

Managing and reducing debt is crucial for financial stability. High-interest debt, such as credit card balances, can become a significant burden during economic downturns. Develop a debt management strategy that focuses on reducing high-interest debt while making minimum payments on other obligations.

Consider consolidating or refinancing debt to secure lower interest rates and reduce monthly payments. Prioritize paying down debt to free up resources for savings and emergency funds. A debt-free or low-debt situation provides greater flexibility and security during uncertain times.

Maintaining Flexibility in Budgeting

A flexible budget allows you to adapt to changing financial circumstances. Develop a budget that can be adjusted based on income fluctuations or unexpected expenses. Categorize expenses into essentials and non-essentials, and be prepared to adjust non-essential spending when necessary.

Track your spending regularly and adjust your budget as needed to align with your financial situation. A flexible budgeting approach helps you manage financial challenges and make informed decisions about spending and saving.

Building a Support Network

Building a support network is essential for navigating unexpected challenges. Connect with friends, family, and community resources that can provide emotional and practical support. A strong support network can offer guidance, advice, and assistance during difficult times.

Explore local community organizations or online groups that focus on financial support or emergency assistance. Having a network of trusted individuals and resources provides additional safety nets and reduces feelings of isolation during a recession.

Preparing for Financial Emergencies

Prepare for specific financial emergencies by creating a contingency plan. Identify potential scenarios, such as job loss or major home repairs, and outline steps to address these situations. This plan should include financial resources, such as savings or insurance, as well as practical steps, such as seeking temporary assistance or finding alternative income sources.

Ensure that all family members are aware of the contingency plan and understand their roles and responsibilities. Having a clear plan in place helps reduce stress and ensures a coordinated response to unexpected events.

Reviewing and Updating Legal Documents

Review and update legal documents, such as wills, trusts, and powers of attorney, to ensure they reflect your current wishes and financial situation. During a recession, it's especially important to ensure that your estate planning documents are up-to-date and accurately represent your intentions.

Consult with a legal professional to review and update these documents as needed. Proper estate planning provides additional peace of mind and ensures that your family is protected and provided for in the event of unexpected circumstances.

Staying Informed and Educated

Staying informed about economic conditions and financial management is crucial during a recession. Keep up-to-date with financial news, economic trends, and changes in government policies that may impact your finances. Educate yourself about financial strategies and resources available for managing economic challenges.

Attend financial workshops, read articles, or consult with financial advisors to enhance your knowledge and make informed decisions. Staying educated helps you navigate uncertainties with confidence and adaptability.

By building a robust emergency fund, creating a comprehensive financial plan, securing adequate insurance coverage, diversifying income sources, managing debt, maintaining budgeting flexibility, building a support network, preparing for financial emergencies, reviewing legal documents, and staying informed, you can effectively prepare for the unexpected. These essential steps provide a foundation for managing financial and family stability during a recession, ensuring that you are well-equipped to handle challenges and maintain resilience through uncertain times.

Home Safety: Beyond the Basics

Home Safety: Beyond the Basics

In times of economic uncertainty, ensuring the safety of your home extends beyond conventional measures. During a recession, financial constraints may limit your ability to address safety concerns, but there are several proactive steps you can take to enhance home safety while managing personal finances effectively. By focusing on both physical and financial aspects, you can create a secure environment for your family amidst economic challenges.

Securing Your Home Environment

A secure home environment is foundational for safety. Begin with basic security measures such as ensuring that doors and windows are properly locked and equipped with reliable locks. Install motion-sensor lights around entry points to deter potential intruders. Simple, cost-effective upgrades like reinforcing door frames or adding security bars to windows can enhance safety without significant expense.

Consider using a home security system with cameras and alarms. While professional systems can be costly, many affordable DIY options are available. Modern smart home technology allows you to monitor your property remotely through your smartphone, providing added security without breaking the bank.

Preparing for Emergencies

Emergency preparedness is crucial for home safety, especially during economic downturns when resources may be limited. Develop a comprehensive emergency plan that includes procedures for natural disasters, fires, and medical emergencies. Ensure that all family members are familiar with the plan and know how to execute it.

Create a well-stocked emergency kit with essentials such as first aid supplies, non-perishable food, water, a flashlight, batteries, and a portable phone charger. Regularly check and update the contents of your emergency kit to ensure everything remains in good condition and within expiration dates.

Financial Safety Measures

Economic downturns can lead to financial instability, making it essential to protect your home from potential financial crises. Review your home insurance policy to ensure it provides adequate coverage for potential risks, such as property damage or loss. Consider increasing coverage for natural disasters or specific threats relevant to your area.

Maintain an up-to-date inventory of your home's contents, including valuable items and electronics. This inventory can be useful for insurance claims in the event of damage or theft. Document items with photos or videos and keep this information in a secure, accessible location.

Energy Efficiency and Cost Management

During a recession, managing utility costs becomes increasingly important. Enhance your home's energy efficiency to reduce monthly expenses. Begin by sealing gaps and cracks around doors and windows to prevent drafts. Insulate your home's walls, attic, and floors to maintain temperature control and reduce heating and cooling costs.

Invest in energy-efficient appliances and light bulbs to further lower utility bills. Many energy-efficient upgrades provide long-term savings that offset initial costs. Regularly maintain heating and cooling systems to ensure they operate efficiently, avoiding unnecessary expenses.

Home Maintenance and Safety Checks

Regular home maintenance is key to preventing costly repairs and ensuring safety. Conduct routine inspections of your home's systems, such as plumbing, electrical, and heating. Address any issues promptly to prevent more significant problems or safety hazards.

Check smoke detectors and carbon monoxide detectors regularly, and replace batteries as needed. Ensure that fire extinguishers are easily accessible and in working condition. Keep fire escapes and exits clear of obstructions to ensure a safe and quick evacuation if needed.

Community Resources and Support

During tough economic times, leveraging community resources can enhance home safety and provide additional support. Connect with local organizations that offer assistance with home repairs, financial aid, or emergency resources. Many communities have programs that provide support for families in need, including services such as food banks, housing assistance, and financial counseling.

Participate in community safety programs or neighborhood watch initiatives to stay informed about local safety issues and support collective efforts to enhance security. Building relationships with neighbors can create a supportive network that contributes to overall home safety and community resilience.

Personal Safety and Health

Home safety also encompasses personal well-being and health. Ensure that your home environment promotes good health practices. Maintain cleanliness and hygiene to prevent illness, and ensure that living spaces are free from hazards that could lead to accidents or injuries.

Consider implementing stress-reducing practices to manage the emotional impact of financial strain. Engage in regular physical activity, practice relaxation techniques, and foster a supportive family environment. Emotional well-being contributes to overall safety and stability, helping your family navigate economic challenges more effectively.

Preparing for Home-Related Emergencies

In addition to general safety measures, prepare for specific home-related emergencies. For example, have a plan for handling plumbing issues, electrical outages, or appliance malfunctions. Familiarize yourself with basic repair techniques and know how to shut off utilities in case of an emergency.

Consider taking basic home repair classes or seeking advice from professionals to enhance your ability to manage minor issues independently. This knowledge can prevent small problems from escalating into more significant and costly repairs.

Maintaining Home Security in a Digital Age

As technology advances, home security now includes digital safety measures. Secure your home's Wi-Fi network with strong passwords and encryption to protect against cyber threats. Be cautious with personal information shared online and regularly update passwords for online accounts.

Educate family members about online safety practices and monitor internet usage to prevent potential security risks. Ensuring digital safety complements physical home security and contributes to overall protection.

By focusing on securing your home environment, preparing for emergencies, managing financial safety, enhancing energy efficiency, conducting regular maintenance, leveraging community resources, promoting personal health, preparing for home-related emergencies, and maintaining digital security, you can effectively navigate home safety beyond the basics. These comprehensive measures help create a secure and stable environment for your family, even during challenging economic times.

Adapting to Change: Flexibility as a Family Value

Adapting to Change: Flexibility as a Family Value

In times of economic uncertainty, adaptability becomes a crucial family value that can significantly impact personal finance and overall family stability. Recessions often bring unforeseen challenges such as job loss, reduced income, or increased expenses, making it essential for families to embrace flexibility and adjust their strategies and expectations accordingly. Here's how families can integrate flexibility into their lives to navigate changes effectively and maintain stability.

Embracing a Flexible Mindset

The foundation of adaptability lies in cultivating a flexible mindset. Encourage family members to view challenges as opportunities for growth rather than insurmountable obstacles. This perspective shift can foster resilience and make it easier to adjust to new circumstances.

Discuss the importance of flexibility in family meetings and set realistic expectations for how each member can contribute to managing changes. Emphasize that flexibility involves being open to new solutions and willing to adjust plans as needed, which helps reduce stress and fosters a supportive family environment.

Adapting Family Financial Strategies

Financial adaptability involves revising and adjusting your financial strategies in response to changing circumstances. Regularly review your budget and spending patterns, especially during times of economic instability. Identify areas where adjustments can be made to accommodate reduced income or unexpected expenses.

Implement a flexible budgeting approach that allows for quick adjustments based on your current financial situation. For instance, if a family member loses their job, reallocate funds from non-essential categories to cover essential expenses. Regularly track your spending and update your budget to reflect changes in income or expenses.

Reevaluating Financial Goals

During a recession, it may be necessary to reevaluate and adjust your financial goals. Short-term goals, such as saving for a vacation or making a large purchase, might need to be postponed or altered. Focus on prioritizing essential goals, such as building an emergency fund or paying down high-interest debt.

Discuss and set new, achievable financial goals with your family, taking into account current circumstances. Revisit these goals periodically and adjust them as needed based on changes in your financial situation.

Encouraging Open Communication

Open communication is vital for adapting to change as a family. Encourage family members to share their concerns, ideas, and suggestions regarding financial and lifestyle adjustments. Creating a supportive environment where everyone feels heard and involved helps build collective resilience and fosters a sense of teamwork.

Hold regular family meetings to discuss any changes in circumstances and the impact on family finances and routines. Use these meetings as an opportunity to collaboratively brainstorm solutions and make decisions that reflect the family's values and priorities.

Adjusting Family Roles and Responsibilities

Flexibility may require redistributing family roles and responsibilities to accommodate changes in income or time constraints. For instance, if one parent loses their job, the other might need to take on additional responsibilities or work longer hours. Similarly, children may need to contribute more to household chores or part-time work.

Discuss and adjust family roles based on current needs and capabilities. Ensure that everyone understands and accepts their responsibilities and feels supported in their roles. Flexibility in roles and responsibilities helps maintain household stability and ensures that the family functions smoothly despite changes.

Exploring New Income Opportunities

Adaptability can also involve exploring new income opportunities or side gigs to supplement family income. Encourage family members to identify and pursue alternative income sources, such as freelance work, part-time jobs, or entrepreneurial ventures.

Consider leveraging existing skills or hobbies to generate additional income. For example, if a family member is skilled in crafting or tutoring, they might offer services locally or online. Diversifying income sources can provide financial stability and reduce reliance on a single income stream.

Implementing Creative Cost-Saving Measures

Creative cost-saving measures can help manage finances more effectively during a recession. Look for innovative ways to reduce expenses without sacrificing quality of life. For example, explore options for reducing utility bills, such as using energy-efficient appliances or adjusting thermostat settings.

Engage the family in brainstorming sessions to identify cost-saving opportunities. Involve everyone in meal planning, budgeting, and finding deals or discounts. Collaborative efforts in cost-saving initiatives promote a sense of shared responsibility and reinforce the value of flexibility.

Building Resilience Through Adaptation

Adaptability contributes to overall family resilience, enabling families to bounce back from setbacks and manage change more effectively. Embrace challenges as opportunities to strengthen family bonds and develop problem-solving skills. Approach changes with a positive attitude and a willingness to adapt, which helps build resilience and confidence.

Celebrate small successes and milestones achieved through adaptability. Recognizing and appreciating progress reinforces the benefits of a flexible approach and motivates the family to continue adapting to changes with a proactive mindset.

Maintaining a Focus on Well-Being

While flexibility is crucial, it's also important to maintain a focus on family well-being during times of change. Ensure that the family's physical and emotional needs are addressed as adjustments are made. Prioritize activities that promote relaxation and bonding, such as family outings, recreational activities, or shared hobbies.

Encourage self-care and support each other in managing stress and maintaining a healthy work-life balance. A well-rounded approach to adaptability that includes attention to well-being helps ensure that the family remains stable and cohesive despite external challenges.

By embracing a flexible mindset, adapting financial strategies, reevaluating goals, encouraging open communication, adjusting roles and responsibilities, exploring new income opportunities, implementing cost-saving measures, building resilience, and maintaining a focus on well-being, families can navigate economic uncertainties with greater ease. Flexibility as a family value not only enhances stability but also strengthens the family unit, allowing it to thrive amidst change.

Health and Wellness: Staying Strong Together

Health and Wellness: Staying Strong Together

During a recession, maintaining health and wellness is crucial for both personal well-being and family stability. Economic stress can impact physical and mental health, making it essential to focus on strategies that support a strong and resilient family. By prioritizing health and wellness, families can navigate financial challenges more effectively and ensure that they remain balanced and unified during tough times.

Fostering a Healthy Lifestyle

A healthy lifestyle forms the foundation of overall well-being and can be a powerful tool for managing stress during economic hardships. Encourage family members to adopt healthy eating habits, which are essential for maintaining physical health and energy levels. Focus on nutritious, cost-effective foods such as vegetables, fruits, whole grains, and lean proteins. Planning and preparing meals together not only promotes healthy eating but also fosters family bonding.

Incorporate regular physical activity into your family routine. Exercise is not only beneficial for physical health but also has positive effects on mental well-being. Engage in activities that the entire family can enjoy, such as walking, biking, or playing outdoor games. Regular exercise helps reduce stress, improves mood, and strengthens family connections through shared experiences.

Managing Stress Effectively

Economic strain can lead to increased stress levels, affecting both physical and mental health. It's important to implement effective stress management techniques to maintain family stability. Encourage open communication within the family to discuss financial concerns and other stressors. Providing a supportive environment where family members can express their feelings helps reduce anxiety and strengthens emotional resilience.

Incorporate relaxation techniques into your daily routine. Practices such as deep breathing exercises, meditation, or mindfulness can help manage stress and promote a sense of calm. Schedule regular family time for relaxation and enjoyment, such as watching a movie together, playing games, or engaging in hobbies. These activities provide a mental break from financial worries and help maintain a positive family dynamic.

Maintaining Mental Health

Mental health is a critical component of overall well-being, especially during periods of economic uncertainty. Encourage family members to prioritize their mental health by recognizing signs of stress or anxiety and seeking support when needed. Open dialogue about mental health helps normalize discussions and reduces stigma, making it easier for family members to seek help.

Consider engaging in activities that promote mental wellness, such as journaling, practicing gratitude, or pursuing creative outlets. Providing opportunities for self-expression and personal growth can enhance mental resilience and overall happiness.

Accessing Healthcare Resources

During a recession, accessing affordable healthcare is essential for maintaining health and wellness. Familiarize yourself with available healthcare resources and services, including community health clinics, telemedicine options, and government assistance programs. These resources can provide access to necessary medical care without placing additional financial burdens on the family.

Review your health insurance policy to ensure that it covers essential services and preventive care. If you are experiencing financial difficulties, inquire about potential assistance programs or sliding-scale fees that may be available. Proactively managing healthcare needs helps prevent potential issues from escalating and ensures that the family remains in good health.

Creating a Supportive Environment

A supportive family environment contributes significantly to overall well-being. Foster a culture of encouragement and empathy within the household, where each member feels valued and supported. Celebrate achievements, no matter how small, and provide reassurance during challenging times.

Encourage family members to support one another's health goals and wellness routines. For example, if one person is working on improving their diet, involve the whole family in meal planning and preparation. By working together towards common health goals, the family can strengthen bonds and create a positive, health-focused atmosphere.

Balancing Financial and Wellness Goals

Balancing financial responsibilities with wellness goals requires thoughtful planning and prioritization. Evaluate your budget to identify areas where you can allocate resources towards health and wellness without compromising essential financial obligations. For instance, invest in affordable home exercise equipment or explore low-cost health and wellness resources, such as community fitness classes or online wellness programs.

Focus on cost-effective ways to promote wellness, such as participating in free community events or utilizing public resources. Many communities offer free or low-cost health screenings, fitness classes, or wellness workshops that can benefit the entire family.

Promoting Healthy Sleep Habits

Adequate sleep is a critical aspect of health and wellness, yet it can be easily overlooked during times of financial stress. Ensure that each family member maintains a consistent sleep schedule and creates a restful sleep environment. Avoid excessive screen time before bed and establish a calming bedtime routine.

Good sleep hygiene contributes to better physical and mental health, improved mood, and increased energy levels. By prioritizing sleep, families can enhance overall well-being and better manage the challenges associated with economic uncertainty.

Cultivating Emotional Support Networks

Emotional support networks play a vital role in maintaining family stability and wellness. Strengthen connections with extended family, friends, and community members who can provide additional support and encouragement. Building a network of supportive relationships offers a valuable resource for emotional and practical assistance during difficult times.

Participate in community groups or local organizations that provide support and resources related to health and wellness. Engaging with others who share similar experiences can provide a sense of solidarity and help alleviate feelings of isolation.

Educating on Health and Wellness

Educate your family on the importance of health and wellness, and involve them in learning about nutrition, exercise, and stress management. Provide resources such as books, online articles, or workshops that offer valuable information on maintaining a healthy lifestyle.

Encourage family members to take an active role in their own health and wellness journeys. By fostering a culture of continuous learning and self-care, families can better navigate the challenges of a recession and maintain overall stability and well-being.

By prioritizing health and wellness, managing stress effectively, accessing healthcare resources, creating a supportive environment, balancing financial and wellness goals, promoting healthy sleep habits, cultivating emotional support networks, and educating on health topics, families can maintain stability and resilience during a recession. A focus on health and wellness strengthens the family unit and ensures that all members are better equipped to handle the challenges of economic uncertainty.

Resource Management: Smart Choices for Scarcity

Resource Management: Smart Choices for Scarcity

In times of economic downturn, resource management becomes critical for ensuring personal finance stability and overall family well-being. When faced with financial scarcity, making smart choices about how to manage resources can help families navigate tough times more effectively. This chapter explores practical strategies for optimizing resource use, making informed decisions, and maintaining stability during periods of economic uncertainty.

Assessing Your Resource Inventory

The first step in effective resource management is to take stock of what you have. Begin by assessing both financial and non-financial resources. Create a detailed inventory of your assets, including savings, investments, and any tangible resources such as household supplies, food, and equipment. This inventory provides a clear picture of your current resources and helps identify areas where adjustments may be needed.

For financial resources, review your bank accounts, retirement funds, and any other investment holdings. For non-financial resources, evaluate your pantry, freezer, and household supplies. Knowing what you have on hand allows you to make more informed decisions about budgeting, spending, and conserving resources.

Prioritizing Essential Needs

In times of scarcity, prioritizing essential needs is crucial. Focus on fulfilling basic necessities such as food, shelter, healthcare, and utilities. Develop a budget that allocates funds primarily to these essential areas, ensuring that your family's most critical needs are met.

Create a detailed spending plan that outlines how much money is allocated to each category of essential needs. Consider any upcoming expenses that may require special attention, such as medical bills or home repairs. By prioritizing essential needs, you can avoid unnecessary expenditures and ensure that your family's core requirements are consistently addressed.

Optimizing Food and Household Supplies

Managing food and household supplies efficiently is a key component of resource management. Start by planning meals based on what you already have in your pantry and freezer. Use meal planning to minimize food waste and make the most of your existing inventory.

Implement strategies for extending the life of food and household supplies. For example, practice proper food storage techniques to prevent spoilage and make items last longer. Consider freezing surplus foods or canning fruits and vegetables when they are in season. These practices help reduce waste and ensure that you have sufficient supplies during periods of scarcity.

Making Informed Financial Decisions

During a recession, making informed financial decisions is essential for managing resources effectively. Review and adjust your budget regularly to reflect changes in income or expenses. Look for opportunities to reduce discretionary spending and find cost-effective alternatives for necessary expenses.

Evaluate your investment portfolio to ensure that it aligns with your current financial goals and risk tolerance. In times of economic uncertainty, it may be prudent to shift towards more conservative investments or explore options for preserving capital.

Exploring Cost-Saving Measures

Implementing cost-saving measures can significantly impact your ability to manage resources during tough times. Identify areas where you can cut expenses without compromising your family's quality of life. For instance, consider reducing energy consumption by using energy-efficient appliances or adjusting thermostat settings.

Explore options for saving on everyday expenses, such as using coupons, shopping for discounts, or buying in bulk. Look for opportunities to negotiate bills or seek out lower-cost alternatives for services such as internet and insurance.

Leveraging Community Resources

Community resources can play a valuable role in managing scarcity. Research local programs and services that offer support during economic hardships, such as food banks, utility assistance programs, and community clinics. Many communities provide resources to help families manage basic needs and reduce financial strain.

Participate in community initiatives or support groups that offer practical assistance and emotional support. Engaging with local organizations can provide access to additional resources and create a network of support during challenging times.

Planning for Long-Term Sustainability

While addressing immediate needs is important, it is also essential to plan for long-term sustainability. Develop a strategy for building and maintaining an emergency fund that can provide a financial cushion during future uncertainties. An emergency fund should cover at least three to six months of essential expenses and be kept in a readily accessible account.

Consider creating a long-term financial plan that includes strategies for debt reduction, savings growth, and investment management. Regularly review and update your plan to reflect changes in your financial situation and economic conditions.

Encouraging Family Participation

Resource management is most effective when it involves the entire family. Encourage family members to participate in budgeting, meal planning, and cost-saving efforts. Foster a culture of financial responsibility and resourcefulness within the household.

Involve children in age-appropriate activities related to resource management, such as tracking expenses or participating in meal preparation. Teaching children about budgeting and resource management helps instill valuable financial skills and reinforces the importance of making smart choices during tough times.

Maintaining Flexibility and Adaptability

Flexibility and adaptability are key components of successful resource management. Be prepared to adjust your strategies and plans as circumstances change. Regularly assess your resource needs and make adjustments to your budget and spending as necessary.

Stay informed about economic conditions and potential changes that may impact your financial situation. By remaining adaptable and open to new solutions, you can navigate periods of scarcity more effectively and maintain stability for your family.

By assessing your resources, prioritizing essential needs, optimizing food and household supplies, making informed financial decisions, exploring cost-saving measures, leveraging community resources, planning for long-term sustainability, encouraging family participation, and maintaining flexibility, you can manage resources smartly during a recession. These strategies help ensure that your family remains stable and well-supported even in the face of economic challenges.

The Power of Community: Finding Support Networks

The Power of Community: Finding Support Networks

In times of economic hardship, the strength of a supportive community can play a crucial role in maintaining personal finance stability and ensuring family well-being. During a recession, leveraging community support networks can provide essential resources, emotional reassurance, and practical assistance. This chapter explores the significance of building and accessing community support systems and how they can enhance resilience during financial challenges.

Understanding the Role of Community Support

A strong community support network serves as a safety net during times of economic uncertainty. It encompasses relationships and resources available through family, friends, neighbors, and local organizations. Community support can range from emotional encouragement and practical help to access to vital services and resources. Recognizing the role that a supportive network plays can empower families to seek out and utilize available resources more effectively.

Building Strong Connections

Building strong community connections begins with active participation in local activities and organizations. Engage with neighborhood groups, community centers, and local events to foster relationships and expand your network. Participation in local events, such as town meetings or volunteer opportunities, provides a platform for meeting others and building meaningful connections.

Create and nurture relationships with neighbors and fellow community members. Simple acts of kindness, such as offering help or sharing resources, can strengthen bonds and create a sense of mutual support. By being an active and engaged member of your community, you can build a network of individuals who can provide support and assistance during tough times.

Accessing Local Resources

Communities often offer a variety of resources that can be invaluable during a recession. These resources may include food banks, utility assistance programs, housing support, and healthcare services. Research local resources available in your area and familiarize yourself with the services offered. Many communities provide directories or online listings of resources that can help families manage basic needs and reduce financial strain.

In addition to formal resources, local community groups or non-profits may offer support programs such as financial counseling, job training, or emergency assistance. Reach out to these organizations to explore available services and determine how they can support your family's needs.

Participating in Support Groups

Support groups provide a space for individuals to share experiences, seek advice, and offer encouragement. During a recession, participating in support groups can provide valuable emotional and practical support. Look for support groups focused on financial management, job search assistance, or mental health.

Joining a support group offers the opportunity to connect with others facing similar challenges. Sharing experiences and solutions with peers can provide insights, alleviate feelings of isolation, and offer practical tips for managing financial difficulties. Many support groups meet online, making them accessible regardless of location.

Leveraging Online Communities

Online communities can be an excellent resource for finding support and information during a recession. Platforms such as social media groups, forums, and online support networks offer opportunities to connect with others, share experiences, and seek advice. Participate in online communities related to personal finance, budgeting, and family support.

Engage actively in online discussions and contribute your own insights and experiences. Building a presence in online communities can provide access to valuable resources, including financial advice, job leads, and emotional support. Be cautious when sharing personal information online and ensure that you are interacting with reputable and supportive groups.

Seeking Professional Support

In addition to informal community support, professional resources can provide valuable assistance during economic hardships. Financial advisors, counselors, and social workers can offer guidance on managing finances, accessing resources, and addressing emotional challenges. Seek out professionals who specialize in helping individuals and families navigate economic difficulties.

Consider accessing low-cost or free counseling services provided by non-profit organizations or community agencies. Professional support can help families develop effective strategies for managing financial stress, making informed decisions, and maintaining overall well-being.

Engaging in Community Volunteerism

Volunteering within your community can strengthen your network and provide a sense of purpose during tough times. By offering your time and skills to local organizations or causes, you contribute to the well-being of others while building connections with fellow volunteers.

Volunteering also provides an opportunity to learn about available resources and support services within the community. Through volunteering, you may encounter organizations that offer additional assistance or support that could benefit your family.

Creating a Family Support Network

In addition to accessing external community resources, creating a support network within your own family is essential. Foster open communication among family members and encourage mutual support. Discuss financial challenges and collaboratively develop strategies for managing resources and maintaining stability.

Establish regular family meetings to address concerns, share updates, and celebrate successes. Building a strong family support network helps ensure that each member feels valued and supported, enhancing overall resilience during economic hardships.

Cultivating Resilience Through Community

Community support networks contribute to family resilience by providing emotional strength, practical assistance, and a sense of belonging. Embrace the power of community by actively seeking out and participating in support networks, accessing available resources, and nurturing relationships with others.

By leveraging the support of your community and creating a strong network of connections, you can better navigate the challenges of a recession and maintain stability for your family. The collective strength of a supportive community can provide the foundation for overcoming financial difficulties and ensuring long-term well-being.

Education and Skill Development for All Ages

Education and Skill Development for All Ages

In times of economic uncertainty, investing in education and skill development becomes a crucial strategy for maintaining personal finance stability and ensuring family well-being. Whether it's enhancing existing skills or acquiring new ones, education plays a significant role in increasing employability, adapting to job market changes, and supporting overall family resilience. This chapter explores the importance of continuous learning and skill development for all family members and provides practical steps for integrating education into your family's strategy for navigating a recession.

Emphasizing Lifelong Learning

Lifelong learning is essential for adapting to the evolving job market and economic landscape. During a recession, the demand for certain skills may shift, making it important for individuals to stay updated with current trends and technologies. Encouraging a culture of continuous learning within the family can help ensure that everyone is prepared to adapt to changing circumstances.

Start by identifying key areas where skills may need updating or enhancement. This could include digital literacy, financial management, or vocational skills relevant to your career field. Emphasize the value of ongoing education and the benefits it brings, such as increased job security, career advancement, and personal growth.

Exploring Online Education and Resources

Online education has become a powerful tool for skill development, offering a wide range of courses and resources that are accessible from home. Explore online platforms that provide courses on various subjects, including coding, graphic design, project management, and financial literacy.

Many platforms offer free or affordable courses, making them an accessible option for families looking to enhance their skills without significant financial investment. Encourage family members to explore these resources and select courses that align with their interests and career goals.

Supporting Children's Education

For families with children, supporting their education is crucial during a recession. Educational attainment is a key factor in long-term financial stability, and investing in your children's learning can have lasting benefits. Support their academic endeavors by creating a conducive learning environment at home and providing necessary resources such as books, educational tools, and internet access.

Engage with your children's teachers and school to stay informed about their progress and any additional support they may need. Encourage them to participate in extracurricular activities and programs that enhance their skills and interests, such as coding clubs, art classes, or sports.

Developing Practical Life Skills

In addition to formal education, practical life skills are essential for navigating financial challenges and maintaining stability. Focus on teaching family members skills that are applicable in everyday life, such as budgeting, cooking, home maintenance, and problem-solving.

Create opportunities for family members to practice these skills through hands-on activities. For example, involve them in meal planning and preparation, teach them basic DIY home repair techniques, and involve them in creating and managing a household budget. Developing these skills helps build confidence and self-sufficiency, which are valuable assets during tough economic times.

Encouraging Career Development

For adults, career development is a key aspect of maintaining financial stability during a recession. Encourage family members to assess their career goals and identify areas for improvement. This could involve pursuing certifications, attending workshops, or gaining additional experience in their field.

Networking and professional development are also important components of career advancement. Encourage participation in industry events, online forums, and professional organizations to stay connected with others in their field and explore new opportunities.

Fostering a Growth Mindset

A growth mindset, characterized by the belief that abilities and intelligence can be developed through effort and learning, is essential for overcoming challenges and adapting to change. Foster a growth mindset within your family by encouraging curiosity, resilience, and a positive attitude towards learning.

Celebrate achievements and progress, regardless of their scale, and view challenges as opportunities for growth. Emphasize the importance of perseverance and adaptability, and model these behaviors in your own approach to learning and skill development.

Utilizing Community and Government Programs

Many communities and governments offer programs and resources aimed at supporting education and skill development. Research local initiatives such as job training programs, educational grants, and community workshops that can provide additional support for your family.

Take advantage of programs designed to enhance employability and career skills, such as job placement services, career counseling, and skills workshops. These resources can provide valuable guidance and support during periods of economic uncertainty.

Creating a Family Learning Plan

Developing a family learning plan can help integrate education and skill development into your daily routines. Set specific goals for each family member, such as completing a certain number of online courses, learning a new skill, or achieving academic milestones.

Create a schedule that allocates time for learning activities and track progress regularly. Encourage open communication about educational goals and challenges, and provide support and encouragement to help each family member achieve their objectives.

Balancing Education with Financial Considerations

While investing in education and skill development is important, it is also essential to balance these efforts with financial considerations. Prioritize affordable or free educational resources and explore opportunities for scholarships or financial aid if needed.

Be mindful of the costs associated with education and seek out cost-effective options that align with your family's financial situation. By making informed decisions and managing resources wisely, you can support education and skill development while maintaining financial stability.

Encouraging Family Engagement

Engage the entire family in the pursuit of education and skill development. Organize family learning activities, such as educational game nights, book clubs, or skill-building projects. Involving everyone in the learning process fosters a supportive environment and strengthens family bonds.

By emphasizing lifelong learning, supporting children's education, developing practical life skills, encouraging career development, fostering a growth mindset, utilizing community resources, and balancing education with financial considerations, families can navigate the challenges of a recession more effectively. Education and skill development not only enhance individual capabilities but also contribute to overall family stability and resilience.

Emotional Intelligence: Understanding and Supporting Each Other

Emotional Intelligence: Understanding and Supporting Each Other

During a recession, when financial pressures and uncertainties mount, emotional intelligence becomes a critical component in maintaining personal finance stability and ensuring family well-being. Emotional intelligence—the ability to understand, manage, and effectively express one's emotions while recognizing and empathizing with the emotions of others—plays a vital role in fostering strong family relationships and navigating the stressors of economic hardship. This chapter delves into the significance of emotional intelligence in family dynamics, offering strategies for enhancing emotional understanding and support during challenging times.

Recognizing Emotional Responses

Economic stress often triggers a wide range of emotional responses, from anxiety and frustration to fear and sadness. Recognizing and acknowledging these emotions is the first step toward managing them effectively. Encourage family members to openly express their feelings and concerns related to financial stress and other challenges.

Create a safe space for open communication where everyone feels comfortable sharing their emotions without fear of judgment or criticism. Practice active listening, which involves fully concentrating on the speaker, understanding their message, and responding thoughtfully. This approach helps validate each person's feelings and fosters a sense of empathy and support.

Developing Empathy and Understanding

Empathy—the ability to put oneself in another's shoes and understand their emotions and perspectives—is essential for building strong family bonds and providing effective support. In times of financial stress, practicing empathy helps family members feel heard and valued, reducing feelings of isolation and misunderstanding.

Encourage family members to actively listen to one another and validate each other's experiences. Practice empathy by acknowledging others' feelings and expressing understanding and support. For example, if a family member is stressed about job loss or financial strain, acknowledge their emotions and offer reassurance and encouragement.

Managing Stress and Emotions

Financial challenges can lead to heightened stress and emotional strain. Developing strategies to manage stress and emotions is crucial for maintaining family stability. Encourage family members to engage in stress-relief activities such as exercise, mindfulness, or hobbies that promote relaxation and well-being.

Incorporate stress management techniques into daily routines, such as regular physical activity, relaxation exercises, and healthy sleep habits. Encourage family members to explore activities that help them unwind and cope with stress in a constructive manner.

Building Emotional Resilience

Emotional resilience—the ability to adapt and bounce back from adversity—is a valuable trait during tough times. Foster emotional resilience within the family by promoting a positive mindset and encouraging proactive problem-solving.

Help family members identify their strengths and past experiences of overcoming challenges. Encourage them to set realistic goals and develop strategies for addressing financial difficulties. By focusing on solutions and maintaining a positive outlook, families can build resilience and navigate financial challenges more effectively.

Supporting Each Other's Goals and Aspirations

In addition to managing immediate financial stress, it is important to support each other's long-term goals and aspirations. Encourage family members to pursue personal and professional growth, even during difficult times. Support their efforts by providing encouragement and practical assistance.

For example, if a family member is pursuing further education or career development, offer support through resources, advice, or time management. Celebrating each other's achievements and progress fosters a sense of unity and motivation, contributing to overall family well-being.

Creating a Supportive Family Environment

A supportive family environment is essential for emotional well-being and stability. Foster a culture of mutual support by regularly expressing appreciation, acknowledging contributions, and celebrating successes. Engage in activities that promote family bonding, such as shared meals, family outings, or game nights.

Encourage open dialogue about financial challenges and work together to find solutions. By addressing issues collaboratively and supporting each other, families can strengthen their bonds and enhance their collective resilience.

Navigating Conflict with Emotional Intelligence

Financial stress can sometimes lead to conflicts and disagreements within the family. Handling conflicts with emotional intelligence involves managing emotions, communicating effectively, and finding mutually acceptable solutions.

Approach conflicts with a calm and respectful demeanor, and focus on understanding each other's perspectives. Practice active listening and empathy to resolve disagreements constructively. By addressing conflicts in a positive and solution-oriented manner, families can maintain harmony and strengthen their relationships.

Enhancing Communication Skills

Effective communication is a cornerstone of emotional intelligence and family stability. Develop communication skills by practicing clear and honest expression, active listening, and nonverbal communication. Encourage family members to articulate their needs, concerns, and feelings clearly and respectfully.

Use positive reinforcement and constructive feedback to support effective communication. Create opportunities for regular family discussions where everyone can share their thoughts and feelings, and work together to address any issues or challenges.

Seeking Professional Support

In some cases, professional support may be necessary to address emotional challenges and enhance emotional intelligence. Consider seeking guidance from a family therapist, counselor, or coach who specializes in emotional well-being and family dynamics.

Professional support can provide valuable insights and strategies for managing emotions, improving communication, and building emotional resilience. If needed, explore community resources or online services that offer counseling and support for families facing financial and emotional difficulties.

Cultivating Gratitude and Positivity

Cultivating gratitude and positivity can significantly impact emotional well-being and family dynamics. Encourage family members to focus on the positive aspects of their lives and express gratitude for the support they receive from each other.

Incorporate practices such as gratitude journaling, where family members regularly reflect on and write about things they are thankful for. By fostering a culture of gratitude and positivity, families can enhance their emotional resilience and maintain a supportive and uplifting environment.

Fostering Emotional Growth

Encourage family members to engage in activities and practices that promote emotional growth and self-awareness. This might include reading books on emotional intelligence, participating in workshops or seminars, or exploring mindfulness and meditation practices.

By investing in emotional growth, families can improve their ability to understand and support each other, navigate financial challenges, and maintain stability during uncertain times.

Emotional intelligence is a powerful tool for fostering family stability and resilience during a recession. By developing empathy, managing stress, supporting each other's goals, and enhancing communication, families can strengthen their bonds and navigate financial difficulties more effectively. Embrace the power of emotional intelligence to build a supportive and resilient family unit capable of overcoming challenges and thriving together.

Creating a Sustainable Home Environment

Creating a Sustainable Home Environment

In times of economic uncertainty, creating a sustainable home environment can significantly enhance personal finance and family stability. Sustainability not only contributes to long-term financial savings but also fosters a sense of stability and self-sufficiency. This chapter explores practical strategies for making your home more sustainable, focusing on energy efficiency, resource conservation, and cost-effective practices that support both financial health and family well-being.

Energy Efficiency Upgrades

One of the most effective ways to create a sustainable home environment is by improving energy efficiency. Start by conducting an energy audit to identify areas where your home is losing energy. Many utility companies offer free or discounted audits that can provide valuable insights into how to reduce energy consumption.

Invest in energy-efficient appliances and lighting. Look for products with the ENERGY STAR label, which indicates they meet high energy efficiency standards. Replacing incandescent bulbs with LED lights and upgrading to energy-efficient refrigerators, washing machines, and heaters can lead to significant cost savings over time.

Insulating your home effectively is another key step. Proper insulation helps maintain a consistent indoor temperature, reducing the need for heating and cooling. Check for drafts around windows and doors and seal any gaps with weatherstripping or caulk. Adding insulation to walls, attics, and floors can also improve energy efficiency.

Water Conservation Measures

Water conservation is an essential aspect of creating a sustainable home environment. Implementing simple changes can help reduce water usage and lower utility bills. Start by fixing any leaks in faucets, toilets, and pipes. Even small leaks can waste a significant amount of water over time.

Install low-flow fixtures such as showerheads, faucets, and toilets to reduce water consumption. These fixtures use less water without sacrificing performance. Additionally, consider using a water-efficient irrigation system for your garden, such as drip irrigation, which delivers water directly to plant roots and minimizes evaporation.

Practice mindful water use by adopting habits like taking shorter showers, turning off the tap while brushing teeth, and using a broom instead of a hose to clean driveways and sidewalks. Encouraging the whole family to adopt water-saving practices can lead to substantial savings and promote a culture of conservation.

Waste Reduction and Recycling

Reducing waste and recycling are important components of a sustainable home environment. Start by minimizing single-use items and opting for reusable alternatives. For example, use cloth bags instead of plastic ones, and choose reusable containers for food storage.

Set up a recycling system in your home to properly sort and dispose of recyclable materials. Educate family members about what can and cannot be recycled and ensure that everyone follows the recycling guidelines. Many communities have curbside recycling programs, but you can also drop off recyclables at local centers if necessary.

Composting is another effective way to reduce waste and create nutrient-rich soil for gardening. Set up a compost bin in your backyard or use a countertop composting container to collect organic waste such as fruit and vegetable scraps, coffee grounds, and eggshells.

Sustainable Food Practices

Adopting sustainable food practices can contribute to both financial savings and environmental sustainability. Start by planning meals and creating a shopping list to avoid impulse purchases and reduce food waste. Use leftovers creatively to minimize waste and make the most of your food budget.

Consider growing your own fruits, vegetables, and herbs if you have space. Home gardening can provide fresh produce and reduce grocery expenses. Even small container gardens or indoor herb gardens can be a valuable addition to your sustainable home environment.

When shopping for groceries, choose locally produced and seasonal items whenever possible. Local produce often has a lower environmental impact due to reduced transportation emissions. Support farmers' markets or community-supported agriculture (CSA) programs to access fresh and sustainable food options.

Eco-Friendly Home Products

Using eco-friendly home products can contribute to a sustainable environment and reduce exposure to harmful chemicals. Choose cleaning products that are biodegradable and free from harsh chemicals. Look for products with eco-friendly certifications or make your own natural cleaning solutions using ingredients like vinegar, baking soda, and lemon juice.

Opt for sustainable materials in home furnishings and decor. For example, select furniture made from reclaimed or sustainably sourced wood, and choose textiles made from organic or recycled materials. Reducing the environmental impact of the products you use in your home can contribute to overall sustainability.

Transportation and Commuting

Transportation is a significant factor in sustainability and personal finance. Reducing reliance on single-occupancy vehicles can lower fuel costs and decrease your carbon footprint. Explore alternative transportation options such as carpooling, biking, walking, or using public transportation.

If possible, consider investing in a hybrid or electric vehicle, which can offer long-term savings on fuel and maintenance. For families with multiple vehicles, evaluate the necessity of each vehicle and consider downsizing if it aligns with your needs and financial goals.

Creating a Sustainable Family Routine

Incorporating sustainable practices into your family's daily routine can reinforce the principles of sustainability and contribute to overall stability. Encourage family members to be mindful of their resource usage and involve them in sustainability efforts.

Create a family sustainability plan that outlines goals and strategies for reducing energy, water, and waste. Involve everyone in setting these goals and tracking progress. Celebrate achievements and milestones to maintain motivation and foster a collective commitment to sustainability.

Budgeting for Sustainable Investments

While some sustainability measures may require an initial investment, they often lead to long-term financial savings. Budget for these investments by prioritizing cost-effective upgrades and focusing on projects that offer the greatest return on investment.

Consider financing options such as rebates, incentives, or low-interest loans for energy-efficient home improvements. Many governments and utility companies offer programs that can help offset the costs of sustainable upgrades.

By implementing energy efficiency measures, conserving water, reducing waste, practicing sustainable food habits, using eco-friendly products, and adopting alternative transportation methods, families can create a sustainable home environment that supports financial stability and overall well-being. Sustainable living not only contributes to financial savings but also promotes a healthier and more resilient family lifestyle.

Planning for the Long Haul: Setting Realistic Goals

Planning for the Long Haul: Setting Realistic Goals

In the midst of a recession, setting realistic goals is crucial for maintaining financial stability and ensuring family well-being. The economic downturn presents unique challenges, but with careful planning and clear objectives, families can navigate these tough times and emerge stronger. This chapter explores practical strategies for setting and achieving goals that support personal finance and family stability over the long term.

Assessing Your Current Situation

Before setting goals, it's essential to assess your current financial situation. Begin by conducting a thorough review of your income, expenses, debts, and assets. Create a comprehensive budget that reflects your household's financial reality, taking into account any changes due to the recession.

Identify areas where expenses can be reduced and prioritize essential expenditures. By understanding your financial baseline, you can set realistic and achievable goals that align with your current circumstances.

Setting SMART Goals

When setting goals, use the SMART criteria to ensure they are Specific, Measurable, Achievable, Relevant, and Time-bound. This approach helps create clear and actionable objectives that are easier to track and accomplish.

Specific: Define your goals with precision. Instead of setting a vague goal like "save more money," specify the amount you aim to save, such as "save $500 per month."

Measurable: Establish criteria for measuring progress. For instance, if your goal is to reduce debt, set a target amount to pay off each month and track your progress regularly.

Achievable: Ensure that your goals are realistic given your current financial situation. Avoid setting overly ambitious targets that may lead to frustration or discouragement.

Relevant: Align your goals with your family's needs and priorities. Focus on objectives that support overall financial stability and address immediate concerns related to the recession.

Time-bound: Set deadlines for achieving your goals. Having a timeline helps maintain focus and accountability. For example, aim to build an emergency fund within six months.

Creating a Long-Term Financial Plan

Develop a long-term financial plan that incorporates your goals and outlines the steps needed to achieve them. This plan should include strategies for managing debt, building savings, and investing for the future.

Consider incorporating the following elements into your long-term financial plan:

Emergency Fund: Establish and grow an emergency fund to cover unexpected expenses or income disruptions. Aim to save three to six months' worth of living expenses in a readily accessible account.

Debt Management: Create a strategy for paying down existing debt. Prioritize high-interest debts and explore options for consolidating or refinancing to reduce interest rates.

Retirement Savings: Continue contributing to retirement accounts, even during a recession. Consider adjusting your contributions based on your financial situation and focus on long-term growth.

Investing: Develop an investment strategy that aligns with your risk tolerance and financial goals. Diversify your investments to mitigate risk and focus on long-term growth.

Involving the Whole Family

Involve all family members in the goal-setting process to ensure collective buy-in and accountability. Discuss financial goals openly and encourage input from everyone. By working together, you can develop a shared understanding of financial priorities and create a unified approach to achieving your objectives.

Assign roles and responsibilities to family members, such as tracking expenses or managing the budget. Encourage regular family meetings to review progress, address challenges, and celebrate milestones. This collaborative approach fosters a sense of teamwork and reinforces the importance of financial discipline.

Adapting to Changes

Flexibility is key when planning for the long haul. Economic conditions and personal circumstances can change unexpectedly, requiring adjustments to your goals and strategies. Regularly review and update your financial plan to reflect any changes in your situation or the broader economic environment.

Be prepared to adapt your goals as needed. For instance, if a family member experiences job loss or a significant income reduction, revisit your budget and adjust your savings and spending goals accordingly. By remaining flexible, you can better manage uncertainties and stay on track toward achieving your long-term objectives.

Monitoring Progress and Celebrating Achievements

Track your progress toward your goals regularly to ensure you remain on course. Use budgeting tools, financial apps, or spreadsheets to monitor your expenses, savings, and debt reduction. Regularly review your progress and make any necessary adjustments to stay aligned with your goals.

Celebrate your achievements, no matter how small. Recognizing milestones and progress boosts morale and reinforces positive financial behaviors. Rewarding yourself and your family for reaching goals can also help maintain motivation and commitment.

Seeking Professional Guidance

If needed, consider seeking professional financial advice to enhance your goal-setting and planning efforts. Financial advisors can provide valuable insights, develop customized strategies, and offer guidance on managing investments, debt, and savings.

Choose a financial advisor with experience in recession planning and a solid understanding of your family's needs. Professional advice can help optimize your financial plan and ensure you make informed decisions.

Maintaining a Positive Mindset

A positive mindset is essential for achieving long-term financial goals, especially during challenging times. Focus on what you can control and take proactive steps to manage your finances effectively. Cultivate resilience and perseverance, and view challenges as opportunities for growth and learning.

Encourage family members to adopt a positive outlook and stay committed to their goals. By maintaining optimism and staying focused on your objectives, you can navigate the recession with confidence and achieve financial stability.

Setting realistic goals and creating a long-term financial plan are vital for maintaining stability and prosperity during a recession. By assessing your current situation, setting SMART goals, involving the whole family, and remaining adaptable, you can build a solid foundation for financial success and family well-being. Embrace the planning process as a means of empowerment and resilience, and work together to achieve your goals amidst economic uncertainty.

Stress Management: Techniques for Family Calm

Stress Management: Techniques for Family Calm

During a recession, stress levels often rise as families grapple with financial uncertainty and its impact on daily life. Managing stress effectively is crucial for maintaining family stability and personal well-being. This chapter explores practical stress management techniques tailored for families facing economic challenges, focusing on strategies to promote calm, resilience, and unity.

Recognizing and Addressing Stress

The first step in managing stress is recognizing its signs and understanding its impact on family dynamics. Common indicators of stress include irritability, fatigue, anxiety, and disrupted sleep patterns. Open communication is key to identifying stressors and addressing them proactively.

Encourage family members to express their feelings and concerns openly. Creating a safe space for discussion helps alleviate feelings of isolation and promotes mutual support. Regular family meetings can provide a structured opportunity to address financial concerns, discuss coping strategies, and reinforce family bonds.

Implementing Relaxation Techniques

Relaxation techniques can help mitigate the physical and emotional effects of stress. Incorporate practices that promote relaxation and mental clarity into your daily routine:

Deep Breathing Exercises: Teach family members deep breathing techniques to calm the nervous system and reduce anxiety. Practice inhaling deeply through the nose, holding the breath for a few seconds, and then exhaling slowly through the mouth. This simple exercise can be done anywhere and helps to center the mind.

Progressive Muscle Relaxation: This technique involves tensing and then slowly releasing muscle groups throughout the body. It helps reduce physical tension and promotes relaxation. Guide family members through a routine of progressively tensing and relaxing different muscle groups, starting from the toes and working up to the head.

Mindfulness and Meditation: Mindfulness practices, such as meditation, can enhance emotional resilience and provide a sense of calm. Set aside time each day for mindfulness exercises, such as guided meditation or mindful breathing. Encourage family members to participate together to build a collective sense of tranquility.

Maintaining a Healthy Lifestyle

A healthy lifestyle supports stress management and overall well-being. Focus on incorporating habits that promote physical health and emotional balance:

Balanced Diet: Encourage a nutritious diet rich in fruits, vegetables, whole grains, and lean proteins. A well-balanced diet supports physical health and stabilizes mood. Involve the whole family in meal planning and preparation to make healthy eating a shared goal.

Regular Exercise: Physical activity is a powerful stress reliever. Aim for at least 30 minutes of moderate exercise most days of the week. Activities such as walking, jogging, or playing sports together can be both enjoyable and beneficial for managing stress.

Adequate Sleep: Ensure that all family members prioritize sleep and establish a consistent sleep routine. Create a calming bedtime environment by minimizing screen time before bed and practicing relaxing pre-sleep rituals, such as reading or listening to soothing music.

Building Resilience Through Routine

Establishing a daily routine provides structure and predictability, which can help reduce stress. Develop a family schedule that includes time for work, chores, relaxation, and recreational activities. Having a routine creates a sense of stability and control, which is especially valuable during uncertain times.

Involve the entire family in creating and adhering to the routine. Set aside time for family activities that promote bonding and relaxation, such as game nights, movie nights, or outdoor adventures. Maintaining a balanced routine helps manage stress and fosters a positive family atmosphere.

Fostering Emotional Support and Connection

Emotional support is crucial for managing stress and maintaining family stability. Encourage family members to support each other through challenging times:

Active Listening: Practice active listening by giving full attention to family members when they share their concerns. Validate their feelings and offer empathy and understanding. Active listening fosters trust and strengthens emotional connections.

Positive Reinforcement: Recognize and celebrate each family member's efforts and achievements. Positive reinforcement boosts morale and reinforces a sense of accomplishment. Express appreciation for each other's contributions and strengths.

Encouraging Hobbies and Interests: Support family members in pursuing hobbies and interests that bring joy and relaxation. Whether it's painting, gardening, or playing a musical instrument, engaging in enjoyable activities provides an outlet for stress and fosters a sense of fulfillment.

Seeking Professional Help

If stress becomes overwhelming or significantly impacts family functioning, consider seeking professional help. Mental health professionals, such as therapists or counselors, can provide valuable support and guidance in managing stress and navigating financial challenges.

Look for professionals who specialize in stress management and family therapy. They can offer coping strategies, facilitate family communication, and help address underlying issues contributing to stress.

Practicing Gratitude and Positivity

Cultivating a mindset of gratitude and positivity can enhance resilience and reduce stress. Encourage family members to focus on positive aspects of their lives and express gratitude regularly. Keep a gratitude journal or create a gratitude jar where family members can contribute notes of appreciation.

Fostering a positive outlook helps shift focus away from stressors and reinforces a sense of hope and optimism. Celebrate small victories and progress, and maintain a hopeful perspective about overcoming challenges.

Creating a Support Network

Building a support network outside the family can provide additional resources and emotional support. Connect with friends, neighbors, or community organizations for social support and practical assistance. Joining support groups or participating in community activities can offer a sense of connection and shared experience.

Implementing Stress Reduction Strategies Together

Involve the whole family in implementing stress reduction strategies to create a collective approach to managing stress. Share techniques and practices that work well for each family member and adapt them to fit your family's needs. By working together, you can strengthen family bonds and foster a supportive environment.

Managing stress effectively is essential for maintaining family stability and personal well-being during a recession. By recognizing stress, implementing relaxation techniques, maintaining a healthy lifestyle, establishing routines, fostering emotional support, and seeking professional help when needed, families can navigate economic challenges with resilience and calm. Emphasizing gratitude and positivity, and creating a strong support network further enhances the ability to cope with stress and maintain a stable and harmonious family life.

Investing in Relationships: Quality Time and Connection

Investing in Relationships: Quality Time and Connection

During a recession, financial pressures can strain family relationships, making it even more crucial to prioritize and nurture connections with loved ones. Investing in relationships through quality time and meaningful interactions not only strengthens family bonds but also contributes to emotional stability and resilience during challenging times. This chapter explores practical strategies for fostering strong connections and maintaining a supportive family environment amidst economic uncertainty.

Prioritizing Quality Time

Amidst the hustle of managing finances and navigating economic challenges, carving out quality time for family is essential. Quality time strengthens relationships, enhances communication, and creates lasting memories. Here's how to prioritize and maximize quality time with your family:

Schedule Regular Family Activities: Establish a routine for family activities that everyone can look forward to. Whether it's a weekly game night, a monthly outing, or a daily shared meal, having scheduled time together provides a sense of continuity and connection. Choose activities that everyone enjoys and that foster interaction and bonding.

Create Family Traditions: Traditions, whether simple or elaborate, offer a sense of stability and continuity. Create or maintain traditions that bring the family together, such as holiday celebrations, special dinners, or annual trips. These traditions become cherished memories and reinforce family unity.

Be Present and Engaged: Quality time is not just about the amount of time spent together but also about being fully present during those moments. Put away distractions like phones and work-related concerns to focus on your family. Engage in meaningful conversations, listen actively, and participate in activities with enthusiasm.

Fostering Open Communication

Effective communication is the cornerstone of strong relationships. During a recession, open and honest communication helps families navigate financial challenges together and supports emotional well-being:

Encourage Open Dialogue: Create an environment where family members feel comfortable sharing their thoughts and feelings. Regularly discuss financial matters, concerns, and aspirations in a supportive and non-judgmental manner. Open dialogue fosters trust and allows for collective problem-solving.

Practice Active Listening: Show genuine interest and empathy when family members speak. Active listening involves giving full attention, acknowledging feelings, and providing feedback. This approach strengthens connections and helps family members feel valued and understood.

Address Conflicts Constructively: Disagreements are natural, but handling conflicts constructively is crucial for maintaining harmony. Focus on finding solutions rather than placing blame. Use "I" statements to express feelings without accusing or criticizing others, and work together to resolve issues.

Engaging in Shared Interests

Shared interests and hobbies provide opportunities for bonding and create positive experiences. Identify activities that resonate with all family members and incorporate them into your routine:

Explore New Hobbies Together: Discover new hobbies or activities that the entire family can enjoy. Whether it's cooking, gardening, or crafting, engaging in new experiences together fosters collaboration and strengthens relationships.

Participate in Community Events: Involve the family in community events or volunteer opportunities. Participating in local activities or charitable projects not only provides a sense of purpose but also creates shared experiences and builds connections with others.

Plan Family Adventures: Organize occasional outings or mini-adventures that offer a break from routine and allow for quality time together. Explore local parks, visit museums, or take scenic drives to create memorable experiences.

Building Emotional Support Networks

In addition to spending time together, building emotional support networks strengthens relationships and provides additional resources during challenging times:

Cultivate Supportive Relationships: Foster relationships with extended family, friends, and neighbors who can offer emotional support and practical assistance. Regularly connect with these individuals to maintain a strong support network.

Engage in Family Support Systems: Create a family support system where each member contributes to and benefits from collective support. Offer encouragement, share resources, and provide assistance to one another as needed.

Seek Professional Support: If needed, consider seeking professional counseling or family therapy to address specific issues or improve communication. A trained therapist can offer guidance and strategies for enhancing relationships and managing stress.

Encouraging Mutual Respect and Appreciation

Respect and appreciation are fundamental to healthy relationships. Promote an environment of mutual respect and recognition within the family:

Express Gratitude: Regularly acknowledge and appreciate each family member's contributions and efforts. Simple gestures of gratitude, such as thank-you notes or verbal praise, reinforce positive behavior and strengthen bonds.

Show Respect for Individual Needs: Recognize and respect each family member's individual needs and preferences. Support each other's goals, interests, and personal space, and strive to balance individual desires with family priorities.

Celebrate Achievements: Celebrate each family member's achievements and milestones, no matter how small. Recognizing and celebrating successes boosts morale and reinforces a sense of shared accomplishment.

Balancing Work and Family Life

Maintaining a balance between work and family life is essential for nurturing relationships. Strive to create boundaries between work and personal time to ensure that family interactions remain a priority:

Set Boundaries: Establish clear boundaries between work and family time to prevent work-related stress from encroaching on family life. Designate specific times for work and family activities, and stick to these boundaries as much as possible.

Practice Work-Life Integration: Find ways to integrate work and family life in a harmonious manner. For example, involve family members in work-related projects or use flexible work arrangements to accommodate family needs.

Take Time for Self-Care: Prioritize self-care to maintain personal well-being and be present for your family. Ensure that you take time for relaxation and activities that rejuvenate you, allowing you to contribute positively to family relationships.

Strengthening Family Bonds Through Shared Experiences

Investing in relationships during a recession involves creating and nurturing shared experiences that reinforce family bonds. By prioritizing quality time, fostering open communication, engaging in shared interests, and building emotional support networks, families can strengthen their connections and navigate economic challenges together with resilience and unity. Emphasizing respect, appreciation, and work-life balance further supports a stable and harmonious family environment, fostering lasting relationships and emotional well-being.

Financial Literacy: Teaching Kids About Money

Financial Literacy: Teaching Kids About Money

As families navigate the uncertainties of a recession, financial literacy becomes an essential skill, not just for adults but for children as well. Teaching kids about money is a proactive step towards ensuring their future stability and resilience. Equipping them with financial knowledge and skills helps them understand the value of money, make informed decisions, and develop responsible financial habits. This chapter explores strategies for imparting financial literacy to children in a way that is engaging, age-appropriate, and relevant to their everyday lives.

Understanding the Basics

Introducing financial concepts at an early age lays the groundwork for a strong understanding of money management. Start with fundamental concepts and gradually build on them as children grow older:

Money as a Concept: Begin by explaining what money is and why it is used. Use everyday examples to illustrate how money is exchanged for goods and services. For young children, use toys or play money to create a simple shopping experience where they can "buy" and "sell" items.

The Value of Money: Teach kids about the value of different denominations of currency. Use visual aids like coins and bills to help them understand how different amounts can be combined to make up larger sums. Practice counting and handling money through games and activities.

Saving vs. Spending: Introduce the concepts of saving and spending. Explain how money can be used to buy things now or saved for future needs. Use a piggy bank or savings jar to visually demonstrate how saving works. Encourage children to save a portion of their allowance or earned money for a future goal.

Setting Goals and Budgeting

Setting goals and budgeting are crucial skills that help children manage money effectively. Teach them how to set achievable goals and create a simple budget to reach those goals:

Goal Setting: Help children identify short-term and long-term goals. Whether it's saving for a toy, a special outing, or a larger purchase, setting goals provides motivation and a sense of purpose. Guide them in determining how much money they need and how long it will take to save it.

Creating a Budget: Teach kids how to create a basic budget to manage their money. Start with a simple budget that includes income (e.g., allowance, gifts) and expenses (e.g., saving, spending). Show them how to allocate money to different categories and track their spending to stay within their budget.

Making Choices: Discuss the importance of making informed choices when spending money. Use real-life scenarios to help children understand the trade-offs between different spending options. Encourage them to compare prices and consider whether a purchase aligns with their goals and priorities.

Understanding Earning Money

Understanding how money is earned is an essential aspect of financial literacy. Teach children about different ways to earn money and the value of hard work:

Allowance and Chores: Introduce the concept of earning money through allowance or chores. Assign age-appropriate tasks that children can complete to earn their allowance. Use this opportunity to teach them about the relationship between effort and earnings.

Entrepreneurial Ventures: Encourage entrepreneurial thinking by helping kids explore small business ideas. They might set up a lemonade stand, offer pet-sitting services, or create handmade crafts to sell. These experiences provide practical lessons in earning money and managing a small enterprise.

The Importance of Work: Explain how different jobs and professions contribute to earning money. Discuss various careers and how individuals earn income based on their skills and responsibilities. This broadens their understanding of how people generate income and contributes to their appreciation of work.

Developing Money Management Skills

Effective money management involves more than just understanding how money works. Teach children practical skills to manage their finances:

Banking Basics: Introduce the concept of banking by explaining how banks work and the benefits of saving money in a bank account. If appropriate, consider opening a child's savings account to teach them about interest and account management.

Using Digital Tools: Familiarize children with digital tools and apps that can help them manage money. Show them how to use budgeting apps or online savings calculators to track their financial goals. Ensure that they understand the importance of online safety and privacy.

Handling Debt: For older children and teens, discuss the concept of debt and the importance of borrowing responsibly. Explain how credit works, the risks of accumulating debt, and the impact of interest rates. Use examples of how debt can affect financial stability and how to avoid unnecessary debt.

Teaching Financial Responsibility

Instilling financial responsibility helps children develop a positive attitude toward money and decision-making:

Modeling Behavior: Children learn by observing their parents. Model responsible financial behavior by practicing good money management, making thoughtful spending decisions, and demonstrating savings habits. Share age-appropriate insights into your financial decisions and how you manage your budget.

Encouraging Philanthropy: Teach children the value of giving by involving them in charitable activities. Discuss the importance of helping others and encourage them to donate a portion of their money to causes they care about. This fosters empathy and a sense of social responsibility.

Promoting Financial Independence: Encourage children to take ownership of their financial decisions. Allow them to make choices about how they spend their money and learn from their experiences. Support them in developing their financial goals and provide guidance as needed.

Making Learning Fun

Engage children in financial literacy by incorporating games, activities, and real-life experiences:

Money Management Games: Use board games or online games that focus on financial concepts. Games like Monopoly or online budgeting simulators provide interactive ways to learn about money management and decision-making.

Practical Experiences: Involve children in real-life financial activities, such as grocery shopping or planning a family budget. Use these experiences as opportunities to teach them about budgeting, comparing prices, and making informed choices.

Educational Resources: Utilize books, websites, and educational programs designed to teach kids about money. Look for resources that present financial concepts in a kid-friendly and engaging manner.

Teaching children about money and financial literacy is a valuable investment in their future. By introducing fundamental concepts, setting goals, and developing money management skills, families can equip their children with the knowledge and habits necessary for financial stability and success. Incorporating practical experiences, modeling responsible behavior, and making learning enjoyable further enhances their understanding and prepares them for a financially secure future.

The Role of Hope and Optimism in Hard Times

The Role of Hope and Optimism in Hard Times

In the midst of a recession, where financial pressures and economic uncertainties weigh heavily on families, hope and optimism can serve as powerful anchors. Maintaining a hopeful outlook and cultivating optimism are not merely about wishful thinking; they are critical components of emotional resilience and stability. This chapter explores how hope and optimism contribute to personal finance and family stability during challenging times, offering strategies to foster these attitudes and harness their benefits.

Understanding the Power of Hope

Hope is a psychological resource that fuels perseverance and motivation. It involves setting goals, having a clear plan to achieve them, and believing in the possibility of success despite obstacles. In the context of a recession, hope plays a pivotal role in maintaining family morale and guiding financial decisions:

Goal Setting and Vision: Hope begins with the establishment of clear, achievable goals. Encouraging family members to set short-term and long-term goals provides a sense of direction and purpose. Whether it's budgeting for essential expenses, planning for future savings, or finding new income sources, having goals fosters a forward-looking mindset.

Positive Expectations: Cultivating hope involves fostering positive expectations about the future. Even in difficult times, focusing on potential opportunities and outcomes helps families remain motivated and engaged. Celebrate small victories and milestones as progress towards achieving larger goals.

Resilience and Adaptability: Hope enhances resilience by providing a mental framework for overcoming challenges. When families maintain hope, they are better equipped to adapt to changing circumstances and find creative solutions to financial problems. Encourage flexibility and adaptability in response to unexpected changes or setbacks.

Fostering Optimism

Optimism, closely related to hope, is the tendency to expect positive outcomes and believe in one's ability to navigate challenges. During a recession, optimism can influence family dynamics and financial strategies in several ways:

Building a Positive Outlook: Develop a habit of focusing on positive aspects of your situation. Encourage family members to acknowledge and appreciate the things that are going well, even amidst difficulties. This practice shifts attention away from negativity and helps build a more constructive mindset.

Managing Stress and Anxiety: Optimism helps mitigate stress and anxiety by providing a sense of control and confidence. Teach family members techniques to manage stress, such as mindfulness or relaxation exercises, and emphasize the importance of maintaining a hopeful perspective.

Encouraging Problem-Solving: An optimistic mindset fosters a proactive approach to problem-solving. Instead of dwelling on obstacles, focus on finding solutions and exploring new strategies. Engage the entire family in brainstorming and problem-solving activities to address financial challenges collaboratively.

The Impact of Hope and Optimism on Family Dynamics

Maintaining hope and optimism can profoundly affect family relationships and overall stability. Positive attitudes contribute to a supportive family environment and enhance collective coping mechanisms:

Strengthening Relationships: Hope and optimism create a positive atmosphere that strengthens family bonds. When family members support each other and share a hopeful outlook, it fosters trust, cooperation, and mutual encouragement. Celebrate achievements and encourage one another through challenges to build a sense of unity.

Enhancing Communication: Optimistic families tend to communicate more openly and constructively. Encourage open discussions about financial concerns and aspirations, and approach these conversations with a solution-oriented mindset. Effective communication helps manage expectations and aligns family members towards common goals.

Promoting Emotional Well-being: A hopeful and optimistic outlook contributes to emotional well-being, reducing feelings of helplessness and despair. Support family members in expressing their emotions and provide reassurance and encouragement to help them maintain a positive perspective.

Practical Strategies to Cultivate Hope and Optimism

Implementing practical strategies can help families nurture hope and optimism during a recession:

Create a Vision Board: Develop a vision board that illustrates financial goals, dreams, and aspirations. Include images, quotes, and reminders of what you hope to achieve. Place the vision board in a prominent location to serve as a daily source of inspiration and motivation.

Practice Gratitude: Regularly practice gratitude to shift focus from financial difficulties to positive aspects of life. Encourage family members to keep a gratitude journal or share things they are grateful for during family gatherings. Gratitude fosters a positive mindset and enhances overall well-being.

Set Up Family Meetings: Hold regular family meetings to discuss financial matters, share progress, and plan for the future. Use these meetings as an opportunity to reinforce hope and optimism by focusing on solutions and celebrating achievements.

Encourage Self-Care: Promote self-care practices that contribute to emotional resilience. Engage in activities that bring joy and relaxation, such as exercise, hobbies, or spending time in nature. Self-care supports a positive outlook and helps manage stress.

Seek Inspirational Stories: Share stories of individuals or families who have successfully navigated financial challenges and emerged stronger. Inspirational stories provide hope and demonstrate that resilience and optimism can lead to positive outcomes.

Navigating Challenges with Hope and Optimism

Hope and optimism are essential elements in navigating the challenges of a recession. By fostering a hopeful outlook and maintaining an optimistic perspective, families can enhance their emotional resilience, strengthen relationships, and effectively manage financial difficulties. Through goal setting, positive thinking, and proactive problem-solving, families can build a supportive environment that helps them thrive despite economic uncertainties. Embracing hope and optimism empowers families to face adversity with confidence and perseverance, contributing to long-term stability and well-being.

Maintaining Routine and Stability

Maintaining Routine and Stability

In the face of a recession, maintaining routine and stability can be crucial for personal finance and family well-being. Economic downturns often bring uncertainty and stress, which can disrupt daily life and affect family dynamics. By upholding routines and creating a stable environment, families can mitigate the negative impacts of financial strain and foster a sense of normalcy. This chapter explores the importance of routines during challenging times and offers practical strategies for preserving stability amidst economic uncertainty.

The Importance of Routine

Routines provide structure and predictability, which are essential for managing stress and maintaining a sense of control. During a recession, establishing and sticking to routines can help families navigate financial difficulties and sustain their emotional well-being:

Emotional Comfort: Routines offer emotional comfort by creating a predictable environment. Knowing what to expect each day can reduce anxiety and provide a sense of security. Routine activities, such as regular meal times or bedtime rituals, help create a stable home life, even when external circumstances are uncertain.

Efficiency and Organization: Maintaining routines improves efficiency and organization. A well-established daily schedule helps manage time effectively, ensuring that important tasks such as budgeting, bill payments, and family meetings are completed consistently. This organization contributes to financial stability by preventing missed deadlines and managing expenses more effectively.

Family Cohesion: Routines strengthen family cohesion by fostering shared activities and bonding opportunities. Regular family meals, weekly game nights, or daily check-ins create a sense of togetherness and reinforce family connections. In times of financial stress, these shared moments help maintain emotional support and solidarity.

Creating a Financially Conscious Routine

Incorporating financial awareness into daily routines can enhance financial stability and promote responsible money management. Here are some strategies for integrating financial practices into your routine:

Budget Review and Planning: Set aside a specific time each week or month to review and update your budget. Regularly assess your income, expenses, and savings goals. Use this time to adjust your spending, track progress, and plan for upcoming financial needs. Involving the whole family in budgeting discussions fosters transparency and shared responsibility.

Expense Tracking: Incorporate expense tracking into your daily or weekly routine. Keep a record of all expenditures and categorize them to identify spending patterns. This practice helps you stay aware of your financial situation and make informed decisions about cutting unnecessary costs or reallocating resources.

Savings Contributions: Allocate a portion of your income to savings as part of your routine. Set up automatic transfers to a savings account or retirement fund to ensure consistent contributions. Establishing a savings habit helps build an emergency fund and provides a financial cushion for unexpected expenses.

Maintaining Routine Amidst Change

During a recession, maintaining routines may require adjustments to accommodate changing financial circumstances. Here's how to adapt your routines while preserving stability:

Adjusting Budgeting Habits: If faced with reduced income or increased expenses, revise your budget to reflect the new financial reality. Prioritize essential expenses, explore ways to cut discretionary spending, and identify opportunities for additional income. Adjusting your budgeting routine ensures that you stay on track and manage your finances effectively.

Modifying Family Activities: Reevaluate and adjust family activities to align with your current financial situation. Explore cost-effective alternatives for entertainment and leisure. For example, instead of dining out, plan home-cooked meals and family movie nights. Finding affordable ways to enjoy quality time together helps maintain family bonds while managing expenses.

Maintaining Flexibility: While routines provide stability, flexibility is also important. Be prepared to adjust your routines as needed to respond to changing financial conditions. For instance, if unexpected expenses arise, you may need to temporarily reduce discretionary spending or reassess your savings goals. Flexibility ensures that you can adapt to new challenges without disrupting overall stability.

Involving the Family

Involving the entire family in maintaining routines and stability enhances the effectiveness of your efforts and fosters a sense of collective responsibility:

Family Meetings: Hold regular family meetings to discuss financial matters, review routines, and address any concerns. Use these meetings as an opportunity to set goals, share updates, and make collaborative decisions. Involving everyone in the process promotes transparency and strengthens family unity.

Shared Responsibilities: Delegate household responsibilities to family members and involve them in routine tasks. Assign age-appropriate chores, such as meal preparation or budgeting tasks, to children or other family members. Shared responsibilities help distribute the workload and reinforce the importance of contributing to family stability.

Encouraging Open Communication: Foster open communication within the family about financial challenges and solutions. Encourage family members to express their thoughts and concerns and provide support and reassurance. Open dialogue helps manage expectations and build a supportive environment.

Maintaining Routine for Emotional Well-being

Routines contribute to emotional well-being by providing a sense of normalcy and stability. Here are additional ways to enhance emotional resilience through routine:

Self-Care Practices: Incorporate self-care routines into your daily life. Prioritize activities that promote physical and mental well-being, such as exercise, relaxation, and hobbies. Self-care routines help manage stress and maintain a positive outlook during challenging times.

Mindfulness and Reflection: Include mindfulness practices and reflection in your routine to enhance emotional resilience. Set aside time for meditation, journaling, or other mindfulness activities that help you stay grounded and focused. Regular reflection on your progress and achievements reinforces a sense of accomplishment and hope.

Creating Rituals: Establish small rituals that bring comfort and joy to your daily life. Whether it's a morning coffee routine, evening family discussions, or weekend walks, these rituals provide a sense of continuity and enhance overall well-being.

Building a Stable Foundation

Maintaining routine and stability during a recession is essential for managing financial stress and preserving family cohesion. By integrating financial practices into daily routines, adapting to changing circumstances, and involving the entire family, you can create a stable and supportive environment. Routines provide structure, foster emotional resilience, and contribute to overall family stability, helping you navigate the challenges of economic uncertainty with confidence and strength.

Effective Communication in Crisis Situations

Effective Communication in Crisis Situations

During a recession, effective communication becomes a cornerstone of family stability and financial management. Economic hardships can strain relationships and create tension, making clear and constructive communication essential. This chapter delves into the strategies for maintaining effective communication within the family during financial crises, emphasizing how transparent, empathetic, and proactive dialogue can enhance personal finance management and support family cohesion.

The Role of Communication in Crisis Management

Effective communication is critical during a recession because it helps manage stress, align goals, and address financial challenges collaboratively:

Reducing Misunderstandings: Clear communication minimizes misunderstandings about financial matters. When family members are informed about financial status, decisions, and plans, they are less likely to misinterpret each other's actions or intentions. This clarity helps prevent conflicts and ensures that everyone is on the same page.

Aligning Financial Goals: Open dialogue allows families to align their financial goals and strategies. Discussing priorities, budgeting decisions, and savings plans ensures that all members understand and agree on the financial direction. This alignment fosters a unified approach to managing resources and navigating economic uncertainties.

Providing Emotional Support: Effective communication provides emotional support during stressful times. Sharing concerns, offering reassurance, and expressing empathy help family members feel supported and less isolated. Emotional support strengthens family bonds and contributes to overall well-being.

Strategies for Effective Communication

Implementing strategies for clear and constructive communication can help families manage financial crises more effectively:

Schedule Regular Check-Ins: Set up regular family meetings or check-ins to discuss financial matters and address any concerns. Use these meetings to review the budget, assess progress, and plan for upcoming expenses. Regular check-ins ensure that everyone stays informed and involved in financial decisions.

Be Transparent: Foster transparency by sharing relevant financial information openly. Provide updates on income, expenses, debt, and savings. Transparency builds trust and helps family members understand the financial situation, making it easier to work together towards common goals.

Practice Active Listening: Active listening involves fully engaging with the speaker, acknowledging their perspective, and responding thoughtfully. Practice active listening during discussions about financial challenges or concerns. This approach helps validate each family member's feelings and promotes mutual understanding.

Encourage Open Dialogue: Create an environment where family members feel comfortable expressing their thoughts and concerns. Encourage open dialogue about financial issues, stress, and emotions. Ensure that everyone has an opportunity to voice their opinions and participate in decision-making.

Handling Sensitive Topics

Addressing sensitive topics related to personal finance requires a careful and considerate approach:

Discussing Financial Difficulties: When discussing financial difficulties, approach the conversation with empathy and understanding. Acknowledge the challenges without placing blame or expressing frustration. Focus on finding solutions and exploring options rather than dwelling on problems.

Managing Expectations: Clearly communicate any changes in financial expectations or plans. If adjustments to spending, savings, or lifestyle are necessary, explain the reasons and implications. Managing expectations helps prevent misunderstandings and ensures that everyone is prepared for potential changes.

Balancing Optimism and Realism: While it's important to maintain a hopeful outlook, also address the realistic aspects of the financial situation. Strike a balance between optimism and realism by acknowledging challenges while focusing on actionable steps and positive outcomes. This approach helps manage anxiety and promotes a proactive mindset.

Conflict Resolution

Financial stress can lead to conflicts within the family. Effective communication plays a key role in resolving these conflicts:

Address Conflicts Early: Address conflicts related to finances early to prevent them from escalating. Discuss disagreements calmly and constructively, focusing on finding common ground and reaching mutually agreeable solutions. Early intervention helps prevent misunderstandings and maintains harmony.

Seek Compromise: When disagreements arise, seek compromise by considering each family member's perspective and finding solutions that address everyone's needs. Compromise fosters cooperation and demonstrates a willingness to work together towards shared goals.

Utilize Mediation: If conflicts become difficult to resolve, consider involving a neutral third party, such as a family counselor or mediator. Mediation provides an objective perspective and facilitates productive discussions, helping to resolve conflicts and restore harmony.

Building Resilience Through Communication

Effective communication not only helps manage financial crises but also builds resilience within the family:

Strengthening Relationships: Open and honest communication strengthens relationships by building trust and understanding. Families that communicate effectively are better equipped to navigate challenges together and provide mutual support.

Fostering Cooperation: Communication fosters cooperation by aligning family members' efforts towards common goals. By discussing financial strategies and decisions collaboratively, families can work together more effectively and achieve better outcomes.

Encouraging Adaptability: Effective communication helps families adapt to changing circumstances. By discussing potential changes and exploring options together, families can respond more flexibly to financial challenges and adjust their plans as needed.

Practical Tips for Effective Communication

To enhance communication during a recession, consider these practical tips:

Use Clear and Simple Language: When discussing financial matters, use clear and simple language to ensure that everyone understands. Avoid jargon or technical terms that may be confusing.

Be Mindful of Timing: Choose appropriate times for financial discussions, avoiding moments of high stress or conflict. Ensure that family members are in a receptive and relaxed state of mind for productive conversations.

Practice Empathy: Show empathy by acknowledging each family member's feelings and concerns. Validate their emotions and provide reassurance and support.

Encourage Positive Reinforcement: Use positive reinforcement to acknowledge efforts and progress. Celebrate achievements and express appreciation for contributions, reinforcing a positive and supportive atmosphere.

Effective communication is a vital tool for managing personal finance and maintaining family stability during a recession. By fostering transparency, practicing active listening, addressing sensitive topics with care, and resolving conflicts constructively, families can navigate financial challenges more effectively and strengthen their bonds. Through open and supportive dialogue, families can build resilience, adapt to change, and work together towards financial stability and well-being.

Cultivating a Positive Family Culture

Cultivating a Positive Family Culture

During a recession, cultivating a positive family culture becomes essential for maintaining both personal finance and family stability. Economic hardships can test relationships and challenge family dynamics, making it crucial to foster an environment where positivity, support, and resilience thrive. This chapter explores how nurturing a positive family culture can help manage financial stress, strengthen relationships, and create a stable home environment amidst economic uncertainty.

The Impact of Family Culture on Financial Stability

A positive family culture influences financial stability in several key ways:

Promoting Financial Resilience: A culture of positivity encourages resilience in the face of financial challenges. When family members maintain a hopeful and proactive attitude, they are more likely to approach financial problems with creativity and determination. This resilience helps families navigate economic downturns more effectively.

Fostering Collaboration: Positive family culture fosters collaboration by creating an environment where family members work together towards shared goals. Collaborative efforts in budgeting, saving, and financial planning strengthen family unity and ensure that everyone contributes to managing financial resources effectively.

Encouraging Open Communication: A supportive family culture encourages open and honest communication about financial matters. When family members feel comfortable discussing their financial concerns and aspirations, they can address issues more proactively and make informed decisions together.

Building a Positive Family Culture

Establishing and nurturing a positive family culture involves several key practices:

Modeling Positive Attitudes: Family members should model positive attitudes towards financial challenges and setbacks. Demonstrating optimism, adaptability, and a problem-solving mindset sets a tone for the entire family. Positive role modeling helps create a culture where challenges are viewed as opportunities for growth rather than obstacles.

Celebrating Achievements: Recognize and celebrate both small and large achievements within the family. Whether it's sticking to a budget, reaching a savings milestone, or successfully managing a financial setback, celebrating these accomplishments reinforces a sense of progress and boosts morale.

Encouraging Mutual Support: Foster a culture of mutual support by actively encouraging and helping each other. Offer reassurance during difficult times, provide practical assistance, and acknowledge each other's efforts. A supportive environment strengthens family bonds and enhances overall stability.

Cultivating Gratitude: Incorporate gratitude practices into your family routine. Encourage family members to express appreciation for each other and for the positive aspects of their lives. Practicing gratitude shifts focus away from financial stress and fosters a sense of contentment and well-being.

Creating a Positive Home Environment

A positive home environment contributes to a stable and supportive family culture:

Maintaining a Positive Atmosphere: Create a positive atmosphere at home by fostering warmth, respect, and kindness. Encourage family members to interact with empathy and understanding, and address conflicts with a focus on resolution rather than blame.

Engaging in Shared Activities: Plan and participate in shared activities that bring joy and connection to the family. Whether it's a weekly family game night, a weekend outing, or a creative project, shared activities provide opportunities for bonding and reinforce positive interactions.

Prioritizing Family Time: Make family time a priority, even amidst busy schedules and financial pressures. Spend quality time together, engage in meaningful conversations, and strengthen relationships through shared experiences. Quality family time enhances emotional support and contributes to a positive family culture.

Navigating Financial Challenges Together

A positive family culture helps families navigate financial challenges more effectively:

Collaborative Problem-Solving: Approach financial challenges as a team. Involve all family members in discussions and decisions about budgeting, spending, and saving. Collaborative problem-solving encourages diverse perspectives and fosters a sense of shared responsibility.

Setting Goals Together: Establish financial goals as a family and work towards achieving them collectively. Whether it's saving for a vacation, reducing debt, or building an emergency fund, setting goals together creates a sense of purpose and motivation.

Adapting to Change: Embrace adaptability within the family culture. Economic conditions and financial circumstances can change rapidly, requiring flexibility and resilience. Foster an environment where family members are open to adjusting plans and strategies as needed.

Promoting Emotional Well-Being

A positive family culture also supports emotional well-being:

Providing Emotional Reassurance: Offer emotional reassurance and support during times of financial stress. Acknowledge each family member's feelings, provide comfort, and reinforce the idea that the family can face challenges together.

Encouraging Self-Care: Support self-care practices within the family. Encourage activities that promote relaxation, stress relief, and personal well-being. Self-care contributes to overall emotional resilience and helps manage the stress associated with financial difficulties.

Building Resilience through Optimism: Cultivate optimism by focusing on positive outcomes and solutions rather than dwelling on problems. Encourage family members to view challenges as opportunities for growth and learning, fostering resilience and a proactive mindset.

Instilling Positive Values

Instilling positive values reinforces a supportive family culture:

Encouraging Responsibility: Teach and model financial responsibility, emphasizing the importance of budgeting, saving, and making informed financial decisions. Instilling a sense of responsibility helps family members develop good financial habits and contributes to overall stability.

Promoting Empathy and Understanding: Encourage empathy and understanding by acknowledging and addressing each other's concerns and needs. A culture of empathy strengthens relationships and fosters a supportive environment.

Embracing Flexibility: Emphasize the value of flexibility in adapting to changing financial circumstances. A positive family culture embraces change with a constructive attitude and seeks solutions collaboratively.

Creating Lasting Impact

Cultivating a positive family culture has a lasting impact on personal finance and family stability:

Long-Term Resilience: A positive family culture builds long-term resilience by creating a strong foundation of support and cooperation. Families with a positive culture are better equipped to handle financial challenges and adapt to changing circumstances.

Enhanced Relationships: Nurturing positive interactions and relationships within the family enhances overall well-being and stability. Strong family bonds contribute to emotional support and a sense of security during times of economic uncertainty.

Sustained Stability: A positive family culture contributes to sustained stability by fostering an environment where financial challenges are managed effectively and family members work together towards shared goals.

Cultivating a positive family culture is essential for navigating the complexities of personal finance and maintaining family stability during a recession. By modeling positivity, celebrating achievements, encouraging mutual support, and creating a supportive home environment, families can enhance their resilience and well-being. A positive family culture not only helps manage financial stress but also strengthens relationships and fosters a stable and supportive home life.

Navigating Financial Aid and Support Options

Navigating Financial Aid and Support Options

In the face of a recession, effectively navigating financial aid and support options is crucial for maintaining personal finance and family stability. Economic downturns often lead to job losses, reduced incomes, and increased financial strain, making it essential to explore available resources and assistance programs. This chapter provides a comprehensive guide to understanding and accessing financial aid and support options that can help families weather economic challenges and sustain their financial well-being.

Understanding Financial Aid Options

Financial aid options vary widely, and understanding the different types of assistance available is the first step in navigating these resources:

Government Assistance Programs: Government programs provide financial aid and support to individuals and families facing economic hardship. Key programs include unemployment benefits, food assistance programs (such as SNAP), housing assistance, and utility assistance. Each program has specific eligibility criteria and application processes.

Nonprofit Organizations: Many nonprofit organizations offer financial assistance, emergency relief, and support services. These organizations may provide help with essential needs such as food, shelter, medical expenses, and transportation. Examples include local food banks, community action agencies, and charitable foundations.

Community-Based Support: Community-based support networks often include local churches, social service agencies, and neighborhood associations that offer financial assistance and resources. These organizations may provide emergency grants, interest-free loans, or referrals to additional support services.

Applying for Financial Aid

The application process for financial aid and support options typically involves several steps:

Research Available Programs: Begin by researching available financial aid programs and support options that align with your needs. Use online resources, government websites, and local community directories to identify programs that provide the type of assistance you require.

Check Eligibility Requirements: Each financial aid program has specific eligibility criteria, such as income limits, residency requirements, or household size. Carefully review these requirements to ensure you qualify for the assistance you seek.

Gather Required Documentation: Prepare the necessary documentation for your application. Common documents include proof of income, identification, proof of residency, and information about your financial situation. Having these documents ready will streamline the application process.

Submit Applications: Complete and submit applications for the financial aid programs you are eligible for. Follow the instructions provided by each program, and ensure that you meet any deadlines for submission. Some programs may require online applications, while others may accept applications via mail or in person.

Follow Up on Applications: After submitting your applications, follow up to check the status of your requests. Contact the program administrators if you have not received confirmation or if additional information is needed. Staying informed about your application status helps ensure timely processing.

Exploring Additional Support Options

In addition to traditional financial aid programs, consider exploring other support options that may provide additional assistance:

Flexible Payment Plans: Some creditors, lenders, and service providers offer flexible payment plans for individuals facing financial difficulties. Contact your creditors to discuss options for deferred payments, reduced interest rates, or modified payment terms.

Debt Relief Services: Debt relief services can assist with managing and reducing debt. Options include credit counseling, debt management plans, and debt consolidation. Seek reputable organizations that offer free or low-cost services to help you navigate debt-related challenges.

Job Training and Employment Services: Many organizations provide job training and employment services to help individuals improve their skills and find new job opportunities. These services may include career counseling, resume writing assistance, job placement, and skills training.

Leveraging Community Resources

Community resources can play a vital role in providing support during tough times:

Local Support Groups: Joining local support groups or networks can provide valuable emotional and practical support. These groups may offer advice, share resources, and connect you with others facing similar challenges.

Educational Workshops: Participate in educational workshops and seminars offered by community organizations. These workshops may cover topics such as financial planning, budgeting, and managing stress during economic hardships.

Volunteer Opportunities: Engaging in volunteer work can provide a sense of purpose and connection. Volunteering with local organizations can also open doors to additional resources and support services.

Staying Informed and Updated

Staying informed about changes in financial aid programs and support options is essential:

Monitor Program Changes: Financial aid programs and support services may undergo changes in response to evolving economic conditions. Stay updated on program changes, eligibility updates, and new assistance opportunities by regularly checking official websites and news sources.

Utilize Online Resources: Use online resources and tools to access information about financial aid programs, application procedures, and eligibility criteria. Many government agencies and nonprofit organizations provide online portals and resources to assist with finding and applying for aid.

Seek Professional Advice: Consider seeking professional advice from financial advisors, counselors, or social workers. These professionals can provide guidance on navigating financial aid options, managing financial challenges, and accessing additional resources.

Preparing for Future Challenges

Preparing for future financial challenges involves proactive planning and resource management:

Build an Emergency Fund: Establishing an emergency fund helps provide a financial cushion for unexpected expenses or economic downturns. Aim to save a portion of your income regularly to build a fund that covers essential expenses for several months.

Create a Budget: Develop a budget to track income, expenses, and savings. A well-structured budget helps manage financial resources effectively and ensures that you are prepared for potential changes in your financial situation.

Review Financial Plans: Regularly review and update your financial plans to reflect changes in your circumstances. Adjust your budget, savings goals, and financial strategies as needed to adapt to evolving economic conditions.

Navigating financial aid and support options during a recession requires a proactive and informed approach. By researching available programs, understanding eligibility criteria, gathering necessary documentation, and exploring additional support options, families can access valuable resources to help manage financial challenges. Leveraging community resources, staying informed, and preparing for future challenges further enhances financial stability and resilience.

Finding Joy in Simple Pleasures

Finding Joy in Simple Pleasures

During a recession, when financial pressures mount and uncertainty looms, finding joy in simple pleasures can be a powerful way to maintain personal finance and family stability. Economic challenges can overshadow everyday joys, but rediscovering and appreciating the small, uncomplicated aspects of life can foster resilience, strengthen family bonds, and promote emotional well-being. This chapter explores how focusing on simple pleasures can provide comfort and stability, even amidst financial strain.

The Importance of Simple Pleasures

Simple pleasures offer a respite from financial stress and contribute to a positive family environment:

Emotional Resilience: Engaging in simple pleasures helps counterbalance the stress and anxiety associated with financial difficulties. Activities that bring joy and relaxation can improve mood and emotional resilience, making it easier to cope with economic challenges.

Strengthening Family Bonds: Shared experiences centered around simple pleasures create opportunities for connection and bonding. Family activities that are enjoyable yet affordable help reinforce relationships and promote a sense of togetherness.

Reducing Financial Strain: Simple pleasures often require minimal financial investment, making them a practical way to find joy without exacerbating financial stress. Embracing low-cost or free activities helps manage expenses while still providing enjoyment.

Identifying Simple Pleasures

Identifying simple pleasures involves recognizing and appreciating the small, everyday experiences that bring happiness:

Nature and Outdoors: Spending time in nature can be a source of great joy and relaxation. Activities such as taking walks in the park, hiking, gardening, or simply enjoying a picnic outdoors offer opportunities for connection with nature and each other.

Creative Hobbies: Engaging in creative hobbies provides a sense of accomplishment and fulfillment. Activities such as painting, crafting, cooking, or writing allow for self-expression and can be enjoyed without significant financial investment.

Quality Time Together: Spending quality time with family members is a fundamental way to find joy. Simple activities like playing board games, having family movie nights, or cooking a meal together foster connection and create cherished memories.

Mindfulness and Relaxation: Practicing mindfulness and relaxation techniques helps manage stress and enhance well-being. Activities such as meditation, deep breathing exercises, or listening to calming music can provide comfort and relaxation during challenging times.

Incorporating Simple Pleasures into Daily Life

Integrating simple pleasures into daily life can be both fulfilling and practical:

Create Rituals: Establish daily or weekly rituals centered around simple pleasures. Whether it's a morning coffee routine, an evening family story time, or a weekend nature walk, creating consistent rituals brings stability and enjoyment to daily life.

Explore New Activities: Experiment with new, low-cost activities to discover what brings joy to your family. Try cooking a new recipe together, starting a family book club, or exploring local community events and free attractions.

Practice Gratitude: Cultivating gratitude for simple pleasures enhances their value and impact. Encourage family members to reflect on and appreciate the small joys in their lives, fostering a positive perspective even during difficult times.

Limit Screen Time: Reducing screen time can help shift focus from financial worries and increase engagement in real-life experiences. Encourage activities that promote interaction and connection rather than passive consumption.

Fostering a Joyful Family Environment

Creating a joyful family environment involves making simple pleasures a priority:

Set Aside Time for Fun: Dedicate time each week for fun, inexpensive family activities. Prioritize activities that everyone enjoys and that promote togetherness, reinforcing the importance of joy in family life.

Celebrate Small Victories: Acknowledge and celebrate small victories and achievements, whether they are related to personal growth, family accomplishments, or financial milestones. Celebrating these moments fosters a sense of accomplishment and positivity.

Encourage Playfulness: Foster a playful and light-hearted atmosphere at home. Engage in activities that encourage laughter, creativity, and spontaneity. Playfulness helps alleviate stress and strengthens family bonds.

Examples of Joyful Activities

Here are some examples of joyful activities that can be enjoyed with minimal expense:

Family Game Night: Host a family game night with board games, card games, or interactive games. Game nights provide entertainment and opportunities for bonding and laughter.

DIY Projects: Undertake DIY projects at home, such as creating homemade decorations, gardening, or building simple crafts. DIY projects promote creativity and offer a sense of accomplishment.

Cooking Together: Cook meals together as a family, experimenting with new recipes or preparing favorite dishes. Cooking together fosters teamwork and creates enjoyable mealtime experiences.

Outdoor Adventures: Explore local parks, nature trails, or nearby landmarks. Outdoor adventures offer fresh air, physical activity, and opportunities to enjoy nature's beauty.

Maintaining Perspective

Maintaining perspective on what constitutes joy can help families navigate financial challenges with resilience:

Focus on Non-Material Joy: Emphasize the value of non-material sources of joy, such as personal achievements, meaningful relationships, and shared experiences. Non-material joys often provide lasting fulfillment beyond financial concerns.

Embrace Simplicity: Embrace simplicity and find joy in the uncomplicated aspects of life. Recognize that happiness does not always require significant financial resources but can be found in everyday moments and experiences.

Adapt and Adjust: Adapt to changing circumstances by finding new ways to enjoy simple pleasures. Be flexible and open to exploring different activities and experiences as financial situations evolve.

Finding joy in simple pleasures is a valuable strategy for managing personal finance and family stability during a recession. By focusing on affordable, meaningful experiences and fostering a positive family environment, families can enhance their well-being, strengthen relationships, and navigate financial challenges with resilience. Embracing simple pleasures not only provides comfort but also reinforces the importance of connection and contentment amidst economic uncertainty.

The Importance of Adaptability and Innovation

The Importance of Adaptability and Innovation

In times of economic uncertainty, such as a recession, adaptability and innovation become crucial for maintaining personal finance and family stability. The ability to adjust to changing circumstances and explore creative solutions can help families navigate financial challenges, seize new opportunities, and sustain their well-being. This chapter delves into the significance of adaptability and innovation in managing personal finances and ensuring family stability during turbulent times.

Understanding Adaptability

Adaptability is the capacity to adjust to new conditions and unexpected changes. In the context of a recession, adaptability allows families to effectively respond to financial pressures and evolving circumstances:

Embracing Change: Recessions often bring rapid and significant changes to the economic landscape. Families that embrace change rather than resist it are better positioned to find solutions and maintain stability. This involves being open to new ways of managing finances, adjusting budgets, and exploring alternative income sources.

Flexibility in Budgeting: Adaptable families regularly review and adjust their budgets to reflect changing financial realities. Flexibility in budgeting includes reassessing spending priorities, cutting non-essential expenses, and reallocating resources to meet immediate needs.

Resilience in Employment: Employment stability may be challenged during a recession, making it essential to adapt to shifts in the job market. Families may need to explore new career opportunities, acquire additional skills, or consider temporary or freelance work to supplement income.

Fostering Innovation

Innovation involves the creation of new ideas and solutions that address challenges in unique and effective ways. In a recession, innovation can play a key role in enhancing financial stability and creating new opportunities:

Creative Problem-Solving: Innovation enables families to tackle financial challenges with creative solutions. This might involve finding new ways to save money, generating additional income through side projects or hobbies, or developing alternative strategies for managing debt.

Exploring New Income Streams: Innovative thinking can lead to the discovery of new income streams. Families might explore online opportunities, start small businesses, or monetize hobbies and skills to supplement their primary sources of income.

Leveraging Technology: Technology offers numerous tools and platforms that can aid in financial management and innovation. Utilizing budgeting apps, investment platforms, and online marketplaces can enhance financial planning and open up new avenues for revenue.

Practical Strategies for Adaptability

Implementing practical strategies for adaptability can help families navigate financial challenges effectively:

Regular Financial Reviews: Conduct regular reviews of your financial situation to assess progress, identify areas for improvement, and make necessary adjustments. This proactive approach ensures that you remain responsive to changes and can adapt strategies as needed.

Emergency Planning: Develop contingency plans for various financial scenarios. This might include creating an emergency fund, setting up insurance coverage, and identifying resources for unexpected expenses. Preparedness helps families adapt more easily to sudden financial changes.

Skills Development: Invest in acquiring new skills and knowledge that can enhance employability and financial stability. Skills development may involve taking courses, attending workshops, or pursuing certifications that align with emerging job market trends.

Encouraging Family Innovation

Encouraging innovation within the family can lead to creative solutions and shared resilience:

Brainstorming Sessions: Hold family brainstorming sessions to generate ideas for overcoming financial challenges. Involve all family members in discussions about potential solutions, budgeting adjustments, and new income opportunities.

Supportive Environment: Foster a supportive environment that encourages experimentation and creativity. Allow family members to explore new ideas, pursue personal projects, and contribute to financial planning with innovative approaches.

Celebrating Successes: Recognize and celebrate innovative solutions and achievements, no matter how small. Celebrating successes boosts morale and reinforces the value of adaptability and creativity in managing financial stability.

Balancing Adaptability and Stability

While adaptability and innovation are vital, balancing these qualities with stability is essential for maintaining overall well-being:

Stability in Core Areas: Ensure that core aspects of family life, such as routine, relationships, and essential needs, remain stable despite financial changes. Stability provides a foundation of security and support amidst economic fluctuations.

Gradual Changes: Implement changes gradually to avoid overwhelming family members. Gradual adjustments allow for smoother transitions and reduce the risk of disruption to daily life.

Monitoring and Evaluation: Continuously monitor the impact of innovative strategies and adaptive measures. Evaluate their effectiveness and make adjustments as needed to ensure that they contribute positively to financial stability and family well-being.

Embracing a Growth Mindset

Adopting a growth mindset enhances adaptability and fosters innovation:

Learning from Challenges: View challenges as opportunities for growth and learning. Embrace setbacks as chances to refine strategies, improve problem-solving skills, and develop resilience.

Continuous Improvement: Strive for continuous improvement by seeking feedback, reflecting on experiences, and staying informed about emerging trends and opportunities. A commitment to ongoing learning and growth supports long-term adaptability and success.

Adaptability and innovation are essential for managing personal finance and ensuring family stability during a recession. By embracing change, fostering creativity, and implementing practical strategies, families can navigate financial challenges with resilience and resourcefulness. Encouraging a culture of adaptability and innovation within the family not only helps address immediate financial concerns but also positions families for long-term stability and success in an ever-evolving economic landscape.

Home-Based Income Opportunities and Ventures

Home-Based Income Opportunities and Ventures

During a recession, when traditional income sources may be strained or unreliable, exploring home-based income opportunities can provide valuable financial relief and stability. Home-based ventures offer flexibility, reduce overhead costs, and allow families to leverage existing skills and resources. This chapter explores various home-based income opportunities and ventures that can support personal finance and enhance family stability during economic downturns.

The Appeal of Home-Based Ventures

Home-based income ventures present several advantages, particularly during a recession:

Cost Efficiency: Operating from home eliminates many of the costs associated with running a business, such as rent, utilities, and commuting expenses. This cost efficiency makes home-based ventures accessible even with limited financial resources.

Flexibility: Home-based ventures offer flexibility in terms of working hours and conditions. This flexibility allows family members to balance work with other responsibilities, such as childcare and household duties.

Leverage Existing Resources: Families can capitalize on existing skills, hobbies, and resources to create income opportunities. Leveraging what you already have can provide a low-risk entry point into new income streams.

Identifying Home-Based Income Opportunities

Several home-based income opportunities can be explored depending on individual skills and interests:

Freelancing and Consulting: Offering freelance services or consulting in areas of expertise can generate significant income. Freelancing opportunities include writing, graphic design, web development, marketing, and consulting in various professional fields.

E-Commerce and Online Retail: Setting up an online store through platforms like Etsy, eBay, or Amazon allows families to sell products from home. This could involve crafting handmade items, reselling products, or dropshipping.

Virtual Assistance: Virtual assistants provide administrative support to businesses and entrepreneurs from home. Tasks may include managing emails, scheduling appointments, data entry, and customer service.

Tutoring and Online Education: Offering tutoring services or creating online courses can be a profitable home-based venture. With the rise of online education, families can teach a wide range of subjects or skills through platforms like Udemy, Teachable, or Tutor.com.

Content Creation: Content creation, such as blogging, vlogging, or podcasting, allows individuals to generate income through advertising, sponsorships, and affiliate marketing. Building a following and creating engaging content can lead to significant revenue.

Home-Based Childcare: Providing childcare services from home can be a viable income source for families. This involves offering care for young children or running a home-based daycare, subject to local regulations and licensing requirements.

Setting Up a Successful Home-Based Venture

Establishing a successful home-based venture requires careful planning and execution:

Market Research: Conduct thorough market research to understand demand, competition, and pricing for your chosen venture. Identifying a niche or underserved market can provide a competitive edge.

Business Plan: Develop a comprehensive business plan outlining goals, target audience, marketing strategies, and financial projections. A clear plan provides direction and helps in setting realistic expectations.

Legal and Financial Considerations: Address legal and financial aspects, such as registering the business, obtaining necessary licenses, and managing taxes. Keep accurate records of income and expenses to ensure financial compliance and facilitate tax reporting.

Professional Setup: Create a professional work environment at home to enhance productivity and maintain a clear boundary between work and personal life. Invest in necessary equipment, such as a reliable computer, high-speed internet, and office supplies.

Marketing and Growing Your Home-Based Venture

Effective marketing and growth strategies are essential for success:

Build an Online Presence: Establish an online presence through a website and social media platforms. Use digital marketing techniques to reach potential customers and build brand awareness.

Network and Collaborate: Network with other professionals and potential clients through online forums, social media groups, and local events. Collaborations and partnerships can provide valuable exposure and new opportunities.

Customer Service: Provide exceptional customer service to build a loyal client base and encourage repeat business. Respond promptly to inquiries, address concerns, and seek feedback to continuously improve your offerings.

Scale Gradually: Start small and scale your home-based venture gradually. Focus on delivering high-quality products or services and expand as demand increases. Scaling gradually helps manage risk and ensures sustainable growth.

Balancing Work and Family Life

Maintaining a balance between work and family life is crucial for the well-being of all family members:

Establish Boundaries: Set clear boundaries between work and personal time. Designate specific work hours and create a dedicated workspace to minimize distractions and maintain focus.

Involve Family Members: Involve family members in the venture where possible. This could include delegating tasks, seeking their input, or working together on certain aspects of the business.

Prioritize Well-Being: Ensure that work does not overshadow family time and personal well-being. Schedule regular breaks, engage in self-care, and prioritize quality time with family members.

Examples of Home-Based Ventures

Here are some examples of successful home-based ventures that families can explore:

Handmade Crafts and Art: Sell handmade crafts, artwork, or custom products through online marketplaces or local craft fairs.

Online Coaching: Offer coaching or mentorship services in areas such as career development, fitness, or personal growth through virtual sessions.

Subscription Boxes: Create and sell subscription boxes filled with curated products or experiences tailored to specific interests or needs.

Digital Products: Develop and sell digital products, such as e-books, printables, or software, that can be distributed online.

Home-based income opportunities and ventures provide a practical and flexible way for families to navigate financial challenges during a recession. By identifying suitable opportunities, setting up a well-structured business, and balancing work with family life, families can enhance their financial stability and resilience. Embracing home-based ventures not only offers a means of generating income but also fosters creativity, innovation, and a sense of accomplishment during uncertain times.

Preparing for Future Challenges: Lessons Learned

Preparing for Future Challenges: Lessons Learned

Navigating personal finance and family stability during a recession requires not just immediate action but also long-term preparation. The lessons learned from managing financial stress and adapting to economic downturns can provide invaluable insights for future challenges. This chapter explores the key lessons families can glean from their experiences during a recession and how to apply these insights to prepare for future uncertainties.

Building a Strong Financial Foundation

One of the most critical lessons learned during a recession is the importance of a robust financial foundation. Families often find themselves unprepared for economic downturns due to insufficient savings or inadequate financial planning. Key takeaways include:

Emergency Savings: The necessity of maintaining an emergency fund becomes glaringly evident during tough times. Establishing and regularly contributing to an emergency savings account can provide a financial buffer against unexpected expenses and income disruptions.

Debt Management: Effective debt management is crucial for financial stability. Reducing high-interest debt and avoiding excessive borrowing helps in maintaining financial health and minimizing stress during economic downturns.

Budgeting Discipline: Creating and sticking to a realistic budget is essential. Families should track their income and expenses, prioritize essential expenditures, and identify areas where they can cut back. Budgeting discipline fosters financial resilience and helps in managing cash flow effectively.

Diversifying Income Sources

The experience of relying solely on a single income source during a recession highlights the importance of income diversification. Families can benefit from:

Exploring Multiple Income Streams: Relying on multiple income streams, such as side jobs, freelance work, or investments, provides additional financial security. Diversifying income sources reduces dependence on a single source and enhances overall stability.

Skill Development: Investing in skill development and education can open up new career opportunities and income streams. Acquiring additional skills or certifications can make individuals more marketable and adaptable to changing job markets.

Entrepreneurship: Home-based ventures and small businesses offer opportunities for income diversification. Families can explore entrepreneurial endeavors that align with their skills and interests, providing an alternative revenue stream.

Strengthening Family Communication

Effective communication is a cornerstone of family stability during a recession. The experience of navigating financial challenges often underscores the importance of:

Open Dialogue: Maintaining open and honest communication about financial matters helps in aligning family goals and expectations. Regular discussions about budgeting, expenses, and financial planning ensure that all family members are informed and involved.

Setting Shared Goals: Establishing shared financial goals and working together to achieve them fosters a sense of unity and purpose. Shared goals create a collective commitment to financial stability and reinforce the importance of collaboration.

Providing Emotional Support: Recessions can strain relationships and increase stress. Providing emotional support and understanding to family members helps in managing anxiety and maintaining a positive outlook during challenging times.

Implementing Effective Stress Management

The ability to manage stress effectively is a crucial lesson learned during a recession. Families often encounter heightened stress levels due to financial uncertainties. Strategies for managing stress include:

Developing Coping Mechanisms: Identifying and implementing effective coping mechanisms, such as exercise, mindfulness, or hobbies, helps in reducing stress and maintaining mental well-being. Families should prioritize self-care and encourage each other to adopt healthy stress management practices.

Maintaining Routine: Establishing and maintaining a routine provides a sense of stability and predictability. Consistent routines help in managing stress and creating a structured environment, even amidst financial uncertainties.

Seeking Professional Support: When stress becomes overwhelming, seeking professional support, such as counseling or financial advice, can provide valuable assistance. Professional guidance helps in addressing emotional and financial challenges effectively.

Adapting to Economic Changes

Adapting to economic changes and remaining flexible is a crucial lesson learned during a recession. The ability to adjust to evolving circumstances enables families to navigate future challenges more effectively. Key aspects of adaptation include:

Monitoring Financial Trends: Staying informed about economic trends and changes helps families anticipate and prepare for potential impacts. Regularly reviewing financial news and market conditions allows families to make informed decisions and adjust their strategies accordingly.

Embracing Technology: Utilizing technology for financial management, such as budgeting apps, investment platforms, and online resources, enhances financial planning and decision-making. Embracing technological tools supports adaptability and innovation.

Being Proactive: Taking a proactive approach to financial planning and risk management reduces vulnerability to economic fluctuations. Proactively addressing potential risks and opportunities positions families for greater stability and success.

Learning from Past Experiences

Reflecting on past experiences and lessons learned provides valuable insights for future preparedness:

Conducting Post-Event Analysis: After navigating a recession or financial challenge, conduct a post-event analysis to evaluate what worked well and what could be improved. Analyzing past experiences helps in identifying strengths and areas for growth.

Documenting Lessons Learned: Documenting lessons learned and successful strategies creates a reference for future challenges. Maintaining a record of experiences and insights ensures that valuable knowledge is preserved and accessible.

Sharing Knowledge: Sharing experiences and lessons learned with others, such as friends, family, or community members, fosters collective resilience and preparedness. Collaborative knowledge-sharing strengthens support networks and enhances overall community stability.

Preparing for future challenges involves applying the lessons learned from navigating personal finance and family stability during a recession. By building a strong financial foundation, diversifying income sources, strengthening communication, managing stress, adapting to economic changes, and reflecting on past experiences, families can enhance their preparedness for future uncertainties. Embracing these lessons not only provides a pathway to resilience but also positions families for greater financial stability and success in the face of future challenges.

Balancing Safety and Normalcy in Daily Life

Balancing Safety and Normalcy in Daily Life

During a recession, achieving a balance between ensuring financial safety and maintaining a sense of normalcy in daily life can be challenging. Families must navigate the dual demands of protecting their financial well-being while preserving the routines and experiences that provide comfort and stability. This chapter explores strategies for balancing safety and normalcy, helping families manage their personal finances and maintain family stability amidst economic uncertainties.

Prioritizing Financial Safety

Financial safety is paramount during a recession, requiring families to take proactive measures to protect their resources and manage risks effectively. Key strategies for prioritizing financial safety include:

Creating a Safety Net: Building and maintaining an emergency fund provides a financial cushion for unexpected expenses and income disruptions. Aim to save three to six months' worth of living expenses to cover emergencies and reduce financial stress.

Reevaluating Expenses: Review and adjust your budget to prioritize essential expenses and identify areas where you can cut back. Focus on reducing discretionary spending and reallocating resources to critical needs, such as housing, utilities, and healthcare.

Securing Income: Explore ways to secure or increase your income, whether through a side job, freelance work, or leveraging existing skills. Diversifying income sources helps mitigate the impact of job loss or reduced earnings during a recession.

Debt Management: Assess your debt situation and prioritize paying down high-interest debt. Effective debt management reduces financial strain and improves overall stability. Consider negotiating with creditors for more favorable terms if needed.

Maintaining Normalcy

While financial safety is crucial, maintaining a sense of normalcy is equally important for family well-being. Normalcy provides comfort and stability, helping families cope with stress and maintain a positive outlook. Strategies for preserving normalcy include:

Establishing Routines: Consistent routines create a sense of predictability and stability. Establish daily routines for meals, sleep, and activities to provide structure and reduce uncertainty. Routines help maintain a semblance of normalcy and support mental well-being.

Fostering Family Time: Prioritize family time and activities that strengthen bonds and create positive experiences. Engage in activities such as game nights, family walks, or home-based hobbies that bring joy and foster connection.

Celebrating Milestones: Continue to celebrate milestones and special occasions, even in modest ways. Birthdays, anniversaries, and achievements can be marked with simple, meaningful gestures that provide a sense of celebration and normalcy.

Maintaining Social Connections: Stay connected with friends, extended family, and community members. Social connections provide emotional support and a sense of belonging. Utilize virtual tools or socially distanced gatherings to maintain relationships and combat feelings of isolation.

Balancing Safety and Normalcy

Finding the right balance between financial safety and normalcy involves integrating both aspects into daily life without compromising one for the other. Consider the following approaches:

Budget-Friendly Activities: Engage in budget-friendly activities that promote normalcy without straining finances. Explore free or low-cost community events, outdoor activities, or creative home-based projects that provide enjoyment and relaxation.

Home Adaptations: Adapt your home environment to support both safety and normalcy. Create dedicated spaces for work, relaxation, and family activities to maintain organization and reduce stress. Make home adjustments that enhance comfort and functionality without significant expense.

Mindful Spending: Practice mindful spending by focusing on purchases that enhance both safety and quality of life. Invest in items or services that provide long-term value and contribute to overall well-being, such as health-related products or educational resources.

Open Communication: Communicate openly with family members about financial decisions and their impact on daily life. Involve everyone in discussions about budget adjustments and priorities, and seek input on maintaining normalcy while managing financial challenges.

Supporting Emotional Well-Being

Balancing financial safety and normalcy also involves addressing emotional well-being. Strategies for supporting emotional health include:

Practicing Resilience: Cultivate resilience by focusing on strengths and finding positive aspects of challenging situations. Encourage family members to adopt a resilient mindset and support each other in overcoming obstacles.

Seeking Professional Support: If financial stress impacts mental health, consider seeking professional support, such as counseling or therapy. Professional guidance can provide valuable tools for managing stress and maintaining emotional stability.

Encouraging Self-Care: Promote self-care practices that support physical and emotional health. Encourage activities that reduce stress and promote well-being, such as exercise, relaxation techniques, and pursuing personal interests.

Long-Term Perspective

Maintaining a balance between safety and normalcy requires a long-term perspective. While addressing immediate financial concerns is essential, consider the following for sustained stability:

Setting Realistic Goals: Set realistic financial and personal goals that align with your current situation. Break down goals into manageable steps and celebrate progress along the way. A long-term perspective helps maintain motivation and focus.

Adapting to Change: Be prepared to adapt to changes and evolving circumstances. Flexibility in financial planning and daily routines enables families to navigate uncertainties and adjust as needed.

Building Resilience: Develop resilience by learning from past experiences and applying lessons learned to future challenges. Resilience strengthens your ability to balance safety and normalcy effectively.

Balancing safety and normalcy during a recession involves proactively managing finances while preserving routines and experiences that support family well-being. By prioritizing financial safety, maintaining normalcy, and integrating both aspects into daily life, families can navigate economic uncertainties with resilience and stability. Balancing these elements enhances overall quality of life and supports family cohesion during challenging times.

Fostering Creativity and Problem-Solving Skills

Fostering Creativity and Problem-Solving Skills

During a recession, personal finance and family stability are often put to the test. The ability to foster creativity and problem-solving skills becomes crucial as families face financial constraints and seek innovative solutions to maintain their well-being. This chapter explores how nurturing these skills can help families navigate economic challenges, optimize resources, and sustain stability.

Encouraging Creative Thinking

Creativity is a powerful tool for overcoming financial obstacles and enhancing family stability. Encouraging creative thinking within the household involves:

Promoting Innovation: Create an environment that values and encourages innovative ideas. Encourage family members to brainstorm and explore new ways to address financial challenges, such as finding cost-effective solutions or generating additional income.

Supporting Hobbies and Interests: Allow family members to pursue hobbies and interests that stimulate creativity. Engaging in creative activities, such as arts and crafts, writing, or gardening, provides a constructive outlet for stress and fosters problem-solving skills.

Celebrating Creativity: Recognize and celebrate creative efforts and solutions. Acknowledging and appreciating inventive approaches not only boosts morale but also reinforces the value of creative thinking in overcoming challenges.

Developing Problem-Solving Skills

Problem-solving skills are essential for addressing financial difficulties and adapting to changing circumstances. Key strategies for developing and applying problem-solving skills include:

Encouraging Critical Thinking: Foster an environment where critical thinking is encouraged. Teach family members to analyze situations, identify underlying issues, and evaluate potential solutions. Critical thinking helps in making informed decisions and solving complex problems.

Practicing Scenario Planning: Engage in scenario planning to anticipate potential challenges and explore possible solutions. Discuss hypothetical scenarios related to financial issues or unexpected events, and work together to devise strategies for each situation. Scenario planning enhances preparedness and adaptability.

Embracing Trial and Error: Encourage a trial-and-error approach to problem-solving. Understanding that not all solutions will be perfect fosters resilience and adaptability. Families should view mistakes as learning opportunities and refine their approaches based on experience.

Utilizing Available Resources

Making the most of available resources involves creatively leveraging what you have to enhance financial stability and family well-being. Strategies include:

Resource Optimization: Evaluate existing resources and find creative ways to optimize their use. For example, repurpose household items, engage in DIY projects, or use resources efficiently to reduce costs and enhance functionality.

Exploring Community Resources: Tap into community resources and support networks. Many communities offer resources such as food banks, financial assistance programs, and educational workshops. Creative exploration of community resources can provide valuable support during tough times.

Leveraging Technology: Utilize technology to support problem-solving and creativity. Explore online tools, apps, and platforms that offer financial management, budgeting, and productivity solutions. Technology can streamline processes and provide innovative solutions to financial challenges.

Fostering a Problem-Solving Mindset

Instilling a problem-solving mindset within the family involves cultivating attitudes and behaviors that support effective problem resolution. Key aspects include:

Promoting Resilience: Encourage resilience by focusing on solutions rather than dwelling on problems. Teach family members to approach challenges with a positive attitude and a determination to find workable solutions.

Encouraging Collaboration: Foster a collaborative approach to problem-solving. Involve all family members in discussions and decision-making processes. Collaborative problem-solving leverages diverse perspectives and enhances the effectiveness of solutions.

Building Confidence: Help family members build confidence in their problem-solving abilities. Provide opportunities for individuals to take on challenges and develop their skills. Confidence in problem-solving fosters a proactive and resourceful mindset.

Adapting to Change

Adapting to change requires flexibility and creative problem-solving. Families should:

Stay Informed: Keep up with changes in the economic environment and adjust strategies accordingly. Staying informed about economic trends and financial developments helps families make timely and informed decisions.

Embrace Flexibility: Be open to adjusting plans and strategies as needed. Flexibility in problem-solving allows families to adapt to evolving circumstances and seize new opportunities.

Seek Continuous Improvement: Continuously seek ways to improve financial management and problem-solving approaches. Regularly evaluate what is working well and identify areas for enhancement.

Cultivating a Culture of Innovation

Creating a culture of innovation within the family involves:

Encouraging Lifelong Learning: Promote lifelong learning and personal development. Encourage family members to pursue educational opportunities, learn new skills, and stay curious. Lifelong learning supports creativity and problem-solving.

Creating a Safe Space for Ideas: Establish a safe space where family members feel comfortable sharing ideas and experimenting. An environment that supports open communication and experimentation fosters creativity and problem-solving.

Recognizing and Rewarding Innovation: Recognize and reward innovative ideas and solutions. Celebrating successes and acknowledging efforts reinforces the value of creativity and encourages continued innovation.

Fostering creativity and problem-solving skills is essential for managing personal finance and family stability during a recession. By encouraging creative thinking, developing problem-solving skills, optimizing resources, and cultivating a culture of innovation, families can navigate economic challenges more effectively and maintain stability. Embracing creativity and problem-solving enhances resilience and provides valuable tools for overcoming financial difficulties and adapting to changing circumstances.

Family Traditions: Keeping the Spirit Alive

Family Traditions: Keeping the Spirit Alive

During a recession, maintaining family traditions becomes a vital component of preserving emotional well-being and fostering stability. While economic challenges can strain finances and disrupt daily routines, family traditions offer a sense of continuity, comfort, and connection. This chapter explores how families can keep their traditions alive during tough times, ensuring that these cherished practices continue to provide joy and reinforce family bonds despite financial constraints.

The Importance of Family Traditions

Family traditions play a significant role in reinforcing identity, values, and connections within the family unit. They offer:

Stability and Comfort: Traditions provide a sense of stability and predictability, offering comfort during uncertain times. Engaging in familiar activities creates a reassuring routine that can alleviate stress and promote emotional well-being.

Shared Memories: Traditions help build and preserve shared memories, strengthening family bonds. Recalling and celebrating these moments can bring families closer together and offer a sense of continuity.

Cultural and Personal Identity: Traditions often reflect cultural heritage and personal values, reinforcing a family's sense of identity. Maintaining these practices helps preserve cultural connections and personal significance.

Adapting Traditions to Financial Constraints

While financial limitations may require adjustments, there are ways to adapt family traditions without sacrificing their essence. Strategies include:

Simplifying Celebrations: Scale back celebrations to fit within your budget. For example, if holiday gatherings are usually elaborate, opt for simpler, more cost-effective versions. Focus on the core elements that make the tradition special.

Emphasizing Homemade and DIY: Create homemade or DIY elements for your traditions. Instead of purchasing expensive decorations or gifts, engage in craft projects, bake treats, or create personalized items together. This approach can be more meaningful and budget-friendly.

Exploring Free or Low-Cost Activities: Identify free or low-cost alternatives that align with your traditions. Enjoying nature, playing board games, or having a movie night at home can provide enjoyable experiences without significant expense.

Maintaining Rituals and Routines

Even during financial hardships, maintaining rituals and routines helps uphold the spirit of your traditions. Consider the following:

Regular Family Meals: Continue to share regular family meals, even if the menu is simplified. Family dinners offer an opportunity to connect, share experiences, and reinforce traditions centered around mealtime.

Seasonal Activities: Engage in seasonal activities that reflect your traditions. Whether it's decorating for holidays, seasonal crafts, or outdoor activities, maintaining these rituals helps preserve the tradition's spirit.

Storytelling and Reflection: Incorporate storytelling and reflection into your traditions. Share stories about past celebrations, family history, or personal experiences related to the tradition. This practice fosters a sense of connection and continuity.

Involving Everyone in the Tradition

Involving all family members in the tradition helps ensure that it remains relevant and meaningful. Strategies include:

Family Participation: Encourage active participation from all family members. Assign roles or tasks related to the tradition, allowing everyone to contribute and feel involved. This collaborative approach strengthens the sense of shared experience.

Creating New Traditions: Introduce new elements or variations to existing traditions that align with current circumstances. For example, if a traditional outing is no longer feasible, create a new at-home activity that captures the spirit of the original tradition.

Celebrating Together: Ensure that celebrations and traditions are inclusive, allowing all family members to participate. Involving everyone promotes a sense of unity and shared purpose.

Communicating the Importance of Traditions

Communicating the value and significance of traditions helps reinforce their importance, especially during challenging times. Strategies include:

Sharing Stories: Share stories about the origins and significance of family traditions. Understanding the history and meaning behind the tradition enhances appreciation and commitment.

Discussing Values: Discuss the values and principles that the tradition represents. Emphasize how these values align with your family's goals and aspirations, reinforcing their relevance.

Encouraging Reflection: Encourage family members to reflect on the impact of traditions on their lives. Discuss how maintaining these practices contributes to family stability and emotional well-being.

Finding Joy in the Simple Aspects

Even during tough financial times, finding joy in the simple aspects of traditions can make a significant difference. Focus on:

Quality Time: Prioritize spending quality time together, regardless of the scale of the tradition. The essence of a tradition often lies in the time spent together and the shared experiences.

Gratitude and Appreciation: Cultivate gratitude and appreciation for the moments shared and the traditions upheld. A positive outlook on the simplicity of the tradition enhances its emotional impact.

Celebrating Achievements: Recognize and celebrate achievements, big or small, within the tradition. Acknowledge and appreciate the effort and creativity involved in maintaining the tradition.

Supporting Emotional Resilience

Maintaining family traditions also supports emotional resilience during difficult times. Consider:

Fostering Hope: Traditions provide a sense of hope and optimism. They remind families of positive experiences and values, helping to maintain a hopeful outlook.

Building Resilience: Engaging in traditions strengthens family resilience by reinforcing connections and providing emotional support. Resilient families are better equipped to navigate challenges and adapt to change.

Keeping family traditions alive during a recession involves adapting practices to fit financial constraints while preserving their essence. By simplifying celebrations, involving all family members, and finding joy in simple aspects, families can maintain a sense of stability and connection. Celebrating traditions enhances emotional well-being and reinforces family bonds, providing comfort and continuity during challenging times.

Coping with Loss and Change

Coping with Loss and Change

During a recession, families may face not only financial difficulties but also significant personal losses and changes. Whether it's job loss, a decrease in income, or the inability to maintain previous lifestyles, coping with these changes requires resilience and adaptability. This chapter explores how families can navigate loss and change effectively while maintaining financial stability and emotional well-being.

Understanding the Impact of Loss

Loss, whether financial, personal, or emotional, can have profound effects on a family's stability. It's important to recognize the various dimensions of loss:

Financial Loss: Job loss, reduced income, or financial instability can lead to increased stress and anxiety. The impact extends beyond immediate financial concerns, affecting long-term plans and family dynamics.

Personal Loss: Losing loved ones or experiencing significant life changes, such as divorce or illness, can deeply affect a family's emotional and psychological state. These personal losses can compound financial challenges, creating additional layers of difficulty.

Lifestyle Changes: Adjusting to a new financial reality may require significant lifestyle changes. These changes can affect family routines, social activities, and overall quality of life, adding to the emotional burden.

Acknowledge and Process Emotions

Acknowledging and processing emotions is a crucial step in coping with loss and change:

Encourage Open Communication: Foster an environment where family members feel comfortable expressing their feelings. Open communication helps in addressing emotions and finding collective support.

Seek Professional Support: Consider seeking professional support, such as counseling or therapy. Professional guidance can help individuals and families process their emotions and develop coping strategies.

Practice Self-Care: Encourage family members to engage in self-care activities that promote emotional well-being. This includes activities such as exercise, mindfulness, hobbies, and relaxation techniques.

Developing a Coping Strategy

Creating a structured approach to cope with loss and change can help manage stress and maintain stability:

Set Realistic Goals: Establish realistic and achievable goals to address the immediate and long-term impacts of loss. These goals should focus on financial recovery, emotional healing, and rebuilding routines.

Create a Budget: Develop a budget that reflects the new financial reality. Prioritize essential expenses and identify areas where adjustments can be made. A well-structured budget provides clarity and control over financial matters.

Adjust Financial Plans: Review and adjust financial plans to align with the current situation. This may involve revising savings goals, re-evaluating investments, or exploring new income sources.

Building Resilience Through Adaptability

Resilience is essential for navigating loss and change effectively. Families can build resilience by:

Embracing Flexibility: Adaptability is key to managing change. Be open to revising plans and expectations based on evolving circumstances. Flexibility allows families to respond effectively to new challenges.

Fostering a Positive Mindset: Maintain a positive outlook by focusing on strengths and opportunities. Encouraging a hopeful and proactive attitude helps in overcoming obstacles and finding solutions.

Strengthening Family Bonds: Strengthen family bonds by spending quality time together and supporting each other. A united family unit provides emotional support and enhances resilience.

Rebuilding and Moving Forward

Rebuilding after a period of loss and change involves taking practical steps to regain stability and confidence:

Develop a Recovery Plan: Create a comprehensive recovery plan that addresses financial, emotional, and practical aspects. This plan should outline steps for rebuilding finances, enhancing emotional well-being, and adapting to new circumstances.

Explore New Opportunities: Look for new opportunities and avenues for growth. This may involve pursuing new job prospects, exploring additional income sources, or discovering new hobbies and interests.

Celebrate Progress: Acknowledge and celebrate progress and milestones achieved during the recovery process. Recognizing accomplishments, no matter how small, fosters motivation and a sense of achievement.

Maintaining Routine and Stability

Maintaining routine and stability is crucial for managing the impact of loss and change:

Establish New Routines: Develop new routines that reflect the current situation. Consistent routines provide structure and stability, helping family members adjust to changes.

Focus on Normalcy: Prioritize activities that promote a sense of normalcy and continuity. Engage in regular family activities and maintain traditions to preserve stability and comfort.

Create a Supportive Environment: Cultivate a supportive home environment that encourages emotional expression and resilience. A positive and nurturing environment helps family members navigate challenges with greater ease.

Finding Strength in Unity

Family unity is a powerful source of strength during times of loss and change:

Support Each Other: Offer support and encouragement to each family member. Understanding and compassion create a strong support network that helps individuals cope with their personal experiences.

Share Responsibilities: Distribute responsibilities and tasks among family members to ease the burden on any single individual. Collaborative efforts strengthen family bonds and enhance resilience.

Stay Connected: Stay connected with extended family and friends for additional support. Social connections provide emotional comfort and practical assistance during challenging times.

Coping with loss and change during a recession requires resilience, adaptability, and a supportive family environment. By acknowledging emotions, developing coping strategies, and maintaining stability, families can navigate these challenges effectively. Building resilience through flexibility, fostering a positive mindset, and finding strength in unity helps families overcome difficulties and move forward with confidence.

Rebuilding and Moving Forward: A Hopeful Outlook

Rebuilding and Moving Forward: A Hopeful Outlook

In the aftermath of a recession, the process of rebuilding and moving forward is essential for maintaining family stability and achieving financial recovery. While the journey can be challenging, embracing a hopeful outlook plays a crucial role in overcoming obstacles and establishing a secure future. This chapter explores strategies for rebuilding after financial setbacks and highlights how a positive mindset can drive progress and renewal.

Assessing the Current Situation

The first step in rebuilding is to gain a clear understanding of the current financial and personal situation. This assessment involves:

Evaluating Financial Status: Review your financial status comprehensively. Analyze income, expenses, debts, and assets to determine the overall financial picture. Identifying areas of concern and opportunities for improvement provides a foundation for planning.

Identifying Key Challenges: Recognize the specific challenges faced, such as job loss, reduced income, or accumulated debt. Understanding these challenges helps prioritize actions and develop targeted strategies for recovery.

Setting Recovery Goals: Establish clear and realistic goals for rebuilding. These goals should address both short-term needs and long-term aspirations, such as reducing debt, increasing savings, or securing stable employment.

Creating a Strategic Plan

A well-structured plan is essential for effective rebuilding and moving forward. Consider the following elements:

Budget Management: Develop a detailed budget that reflects your current financial situation. Allocate resources to essential expenses, prioritize debt repayment, and identify areas where savings can be made. Regularly review and adjust the budget as circumstances change.

Debt Reduction: Focus on reducing and managing debt. Explore options such as debt consolidation, negotiation with creditors, or creating a repayment plan. Prioritize high-interest debts to minimize financial strain.

Emergency Fund: Rebuild or establish an emergency fund to provide financial security in case of unexpected expenses. Aim to save a portion of your income regularly to create a safety net that supports stability during uncertain times.

Exploring New Opportunities

Rebuilding often involves exploring new opportunities for growth and income. Strategies include:

Career Development: Seek opportunities for career advancement or transition. Consider upskilling or reskilling to enhance employability and open new job prospects. Networking and professional development can lead to valuable opportunities.

Alternative Income Sources: Explore alternative income sources, such as freelancing, part-time work, or home-based ventures. Diversifying income streams can provide additional financial stability and reduce reliance on a single source of income.

Investment in Skills: Invest in skills and education that can lead to new opportunities. This may include enrolling in courses, attending workshops, or gaining certifications relevant to emerging fields.

Maintaining a Positive Mindset

A hopeful outlook is a powerful tool for navigating the rebuilding process. Strategies for maintaining positivity include:

Focus on Achievements: Celebrate small victories and milestones along the way. Recognizing progress, no matter how incremental, boosts morale and reinforces a sense of accomplishment.

Practice Gratitude: Cultivate a practice of gratitude by acknowledging the positives in your life. Expressing appreciation for what you have can shift focus away from challenges and foster a more optimistic outlook.

Visualize Success: Engage in visualization techniques to imagine successful outcomes and the realization of goals. Visualizing success can enhance motivation and resilience, helping you stay focused on positive results.

Strengthening Family Bonds

Family support plays a crucial role in the rebuilding process. Strengthen family bonds by:

Fostering Open Communication: Maintain open lines of communication within the family. Discuss challenges, progress, and plans openly to ensure that everyone is informed and involved in the recovery process.

Offering Support: Provide emotional and practical support to family members. A supportive environment enhances resilience and fosters a sense of unity during difficult times.

Setting Shared Goals: Establish shared goals and work together towards achieving them. Collaborative efforts in goal-setting and problem-solving strengthen family cohesion and create a sense of shared purpose.

Building Long-Term Resilience

Rebuilding and moving forward also involves preparing for future challenges and building long-term resilience:

Develop a Contingency Plan: Create a contingency plan to address potential future setbacks. Having a plan in place provides a sense of preparedness and reduces anxiety about the unknown.

Adapt and Innovate: Embrace adaptability and innovation as key components of resilience. Be open to new approaches and solutions that can enhance financial stability and family well-being.

Seek Continuous Improvement: Commit to continuous improvement in financial management and personal development. Regularly review and adjust strategies to ensure ongoing progress and stability.

Celebrating Progress and Growth

Recognize and celebrate progress throughout the rebuilding journey. Acknowledging achievements and milestones reinforces a sense of accomplishment and motivates continued effort.

Mark Milestones: Celebrate significant milestones and achievements in the rebuilding process. Whether it's reaching a financial goal, securing new employment, or achieving personal growth, marking these moments reinforces positive progress.

Reflect on Growth: Reflect on personal and family growth experienced during the recovery process. Understanding how challenges have led to increased resilience and strength provides a sense of fulfillment and hope.

Rebuilding and moving forward after a recession requires a combination of strategic planning, positivity, and family support. By assessing the current situation, creating a strategic plan, exploring new opportunities, and maintaining a hopeful outlook, families can navigate financial challenges effectively. Strengthening family bonds, building long-term resilience, and celebrating progress contribute to a successful recovery and a secure future.

Quick Tips

- Create a Family Budget: Track income and expenses to manage money effectively.
- Cut Unnecessary Expenses: Identify and eliminate non-essential spending.
- Build an Emergency Fund: Save at least 3-6 months' worth of expenses.
- Reduce Debt: Focus on paying down high-interest debt.
- Plan Meals: Plan and prepare meals to avoid waste and save money.
- Shop Smart: Use coupons, buy in bulk, and seek out sales.
- Increase Savings: Allocate a portion of your income to savings regularly.
- Diversify Income: Explore side gigs or freelance work for additional income.
- Review Subscriptions: Cancel or pause subscriptions you don't use.
- Strengthen Family Communication: Discuss financial situations and goals openly.
- Prioritize Essentials: Focus spending on needs rather than wants.
- DIY Projects: Tackle home repairs and improvements yourself when possible.
- Optimize Energy Use: Implement energy-saving measures to reduce utility bills.
- Educate on Financial Literacy: Teach children about budgeting and saving.
- Negotiate Bills: Contact service providers to negotiate lower rates or payment plans.
- Seek Financial Aid: Explore government assistance programs and community resources.

- Foster a Positive Outlook: Maintain a hopeful and proactive mindset.
- Engage in Free Activities: Find free or low-cost entertainment and recreational activities.
- Use Public Resources: Utilize libraries and community centers for educational and leisure activities.
- Invest in Health: Maintain a healthy lifestyle to avoid costly medical expenses.
- Practice Stress Management: Use techniques like meditation or exercise to manage stress.
- Strengthen Support Networks: Build connections with friends, family, and community groups.
- Plan for Long-Term Goals: Set realistic financial and personal goals for recovery.
- Stay Informed: Keep up-to-date with economic news and financial advice.
- Teach Problem-Solving: Encourage creative solutions for financial challenges.
- Maintain Routine: Establish and stick to daily routines for stability.
- Adopt a Flexible Attitude: Be open to adjusting plans and strategies as needed.
- Create a Crisis Plan: Develop a plan for unexpected emergencies or financial setbacks.
- Encourage Family Bonding: Spend quality time together to strengthen relationships.
- Review Insurance Coverage: Ensure you have adequate insurance to cover potential risks.
- Stay Organized: Keep track of important documents and financial records.
- Participate in Community Events: Engage in local events and activities to build connections.

- Limit Eating Out: Prepare meals at home to save money.
- Plan for Education: Look for affordable or free educational resources and opportunities.
- Be Proactive with Health Care: Schedule regular check-ups to prevent major issues.
- Seek Counseling: Get professional help if needed to manage emotional stress.
- Set Up Automatic Savings: Use automatic transfers to grow savings effortlessly.
- Participate in Bartering: Exchange goods or services with others to save money.
- Monitor Spending: Regularly review and adjust your budget as needed.
- Foster Creativity: Encourage creative problem-solving and innovative thinking.
- Explore Home-Based Opportunities: Look for ways to earn income from home.
- Attend Workshops: Participate in financial literacy and personal development workshops.
- Leverage Technology: Use apps and tools for budgeting and expense tracking.
- Revisit Financial Goals: Adjust goals based on current financial realities.
- Encourage Volunteerism: Get involved in community service to strengthen connections and give back.
- Implement Cost-Cutting Measures: Find ways to reduce everyday expenses.
- Stay Physically Active: Engage in regular physical activity to maintain health.
- Monitor Credit Reports: Regularly check and manage your credit report and score.
- Practice Mindfulness: Use mindfulness techniques to stay

grounded and focused.

- Set Realistic Expectations: Be realistic about what can be achieved financially.
- Plan for Seasonal Expenses: Prepare for annual expenses like holidays or back-to-school.
- Reduce Discretionary Spending: Cut back on luxury or non-essential items.
- Develop a Support System: Build a network of friends and family for emotional support.
- Use Online Resources: Take advantage of online tools for financial planning and budgeting.
- Maintain a Positive Attitude: Focus on what can be controlled and celebrate small victories.
- Encourage Family Involvement: Get all family members involved in managing finances.
- Seek Professional Advice: Consult financial advisors or counselors for guidance.
- Participate in Skill-Building Activities: Engage in activities that improve personal and professional skills.
- Evaluate Housing Costs: Consider refinancing or downsizing to reduce housing expenses.
- Review and Adjust Investments: Reassess investment strategies based on current economic conditions.
- Create a Financial Safety Net: Ensure you have backup plans for potential emergencies.
- Foster a Growth Mindset: Embrace challenges as opportunities for growth.
- Engage in Family Projects: Work on projects together to strengthen relationships and achieve goals.
- Monitor Market Trends: Stay informed about market trends and economic forecasts.
- Encourage Open Dialogue: Foster an environment where

family members feel comfortable discussing finances.
- Plan for Retirement: Continue contributing to retirement plans, even if in smaller amounts.
- Be Adaptable: Adjust plans and strategies based on changing circumstances.
- Utilize Community Services: Take advantage of local community services and resources.
- Set Priorities: Focus on essential needs and prioritize financial obligations.
- Encourage Family Resilience: Support each other in developing resilience and adaptability.
- Explore Tax Benefits: Utilize available tax credits and deductions to reduce tax liabilities.
- Plan for Long-Term Security: Develop a plan for long-term financial security and stability.
- Maintain a Healthy Lifestyle: Invest in health and wellness to prevent costly medical issues.
- Review Financial Statements: Regularly review bank and credit card statements for accuracy.
- Seek Cost-Free Activities: Find low-cost or free activities for family enjoyment.
- Set Short-Term Goals: Focus on achievable short-term goals to build momentum.
- Foster Family Creativity: Engage in creative activities to strengthen family bonds.
- Explore Scholarships and Grants: Look for educational scholarships and grants for family members.
- Practice Frugality: Adopt a frugal mindset to maximize resources and minimize waste.
- Encourage Lifelong Learning: Promote continuous learning and personal development.
- Seek Financial Counseling: Obtain advice from financial

counselors to manage debt and improve finances.

- Participate in Local Exchanges: Join local exchange programs for goods and services.
- Evaluate Insurance Needs: Review and adjust insurance coverage to ensure adequate protection.
- Stay Connected: Maintain connections with friends and family for emotional support.
- Manage Stress Effectively: Use stress management techniques to maintain mental well-being.
- Explore Government Programs: Research and apply for government assistance programs.
- Encourage Savings Habits: Instill good savings habits in all family members.
- Review and Adjust Goals Regularly: Periodically reassess and update financial and personal goals.
- Participate in Community Support Groups: Engage with support groups for shared experiences and advice.
- Monitor Household Expenses: Keep track of household expenses and find ways to cut costs.
- Plan for Emergencies: Develop a comprehensive emergency plan for various scenarios.
- Promote Family Involvement: Encourage all family members to participate in financial planning.
- Seek Out Educational Resources: Utilize free or low-cost educational resources for self-improvement.
- Balance Work and Family Life: Maintain a healthy balance between work responsibilities and family time.
- Review Financial Goals: Regularly review and adjust financial goals based on current circumstances.
- Participate in Free Webinars: Attend free webinars for financial education and advice.
- Encourage Positive Thinking: Foster a positive mindset to

overcome challenges and setbacks.

- Create a Home Inventory: Maintain an inventory of household items for insurance and organization.
- Utilize Financial Apps: Use apps to track expenses, manage budgets, and monitor financial goals.
- Celebrate Progress: Acknowledge and celebrate financial milestones and achievements.

Get Another Book Free

We love writing and have produced many books.

As a thank you for being one of our amazing readers, we'd like to offer you a free book.

To claim this limited-time offer, visit the site below and enter your name and email address.

You'll receive one of our great books directly to your email, completely free!

https://free.copypeople.com

---

1. https://free.copypeople.com

Don't miss out!

Visit the website below and you can sign up to receive emails whenever CopyPeople publishes a new book. There's no charge and no obligation.

https://books2read.com/r/B-A-IWAPB-UPBUE

BOOKS 2 READ

Connecting independent readers to independent writers.

Did you love *Protecting & Prospering In Uncertain Times*? Then you should read *Short Selling and Dark Pool Volume: Navigating the Shadows of the Market*[2] by AUMANGEA GROUP LIMITED!

Embark on a journey through the complex and often concealed world of short selling and dark pool trading with "Short Selling and Dark Pool Volume: Navigating the Shadows of the Market." This definitive guide is designed for both beginners eager to understand the fundamentals and experienced traders aiming to master advanced strategies.

---

2. https://books2read.com/u/3y2pEe

3. https://books2read.com/u/3y2pEe

Unveil the Hidden Mechanics of Market Movements: Gain a comprehensive understanding of how short selling works, its strategic purposes, and the step-by-step processes involved. Learn from both historical legends like Jesse Livermore and contemporary phenomena such as the GameStop (GME) squeeze.

Learn from Real-World Examples: Delve into detailed case studies including the collapses of Enron and Lehman Brothers, the dramatic rise and fall of Volkswagen's stock, and the controversial trades involving Tesla and Herbalife. These examples highlight both spectacular successes and sobering failures.

Master Advanced Strategies and Tools: Equip yourself with cutting-edge techniques in algorithmic trading, sentiment analysis, and the utilization of dark pools. Discover how to leverage these sophisticated tools and platforms to enhance your trading strategies and manage risk effectively.

Stay Ahead of Emerging Trends: Explore the future landscape of short selling and dark pool trading, the significant role of retail investors, and the potential for another "Mother of All Short Squeezes" (MOASS). Stay informed about the latest trends and technological advancements shaping the financial markets.

Expert Advice and Legal Insights: Navigate the intricate legal and ethical dimensions of short selling with expert guidance on compliance, transparency, and ethical conduct. Learn the importance of disclaimers, data protection, and maintaining market integrity.

Whether your goal is to safeguard your portfolio during market downturns or to capitalize on declining stock prices, "Short Selling and Dark Pool Volume: Navigating the Shadows of the Market" offers the knowledge and tools necessary for success. Join the ranks of well-informed traders who turn market complexities into opportunities.

Start mastering the shadows of the market today!

Also by CopyPeople

Short Selling and Dark Pool Volume: Navigating the Shadows of the
Market
Understanding Your Pelvic Floor
Protecting & Prospering In Uncertain Times